For God's Sake, Be Human

For God's Sake, Be Human

John Killinger

WORD BOOKS, Publisher
Waco, Texas—London, England

Library of Congress Catalog Card Number: 77–
111961

Grateful acknowledgment is made to the Division
of Christian Education of the National Council
of the Churches of Christ for permission to quote
from The Revised Standard Version of the Bible,
copyright 1946 and 1952.

With love and admiration for

ANNIE

who is the real expert

on being human

Contents

Introduction

THERE IS WIDESPREAD AGREEMENT today that man is passing through an unprecedented crisis in his identity. In every aspect of life—politics, ethics, education, the arts, the sciences, even religion—there is revolution. Nothing is the same anymore. In the words of a character in Marc Connelly's play *Green Pastures*, "Everything nailed down is comin' loose."

There is good reason for such a crisis. We have been confessing for over a century now that we no longer have a central theological vision. There is a crisis of faith, in other words. Melville and Nietzsche and Dostoevsky and at least a dozen other prophetic figures were writing of it well before our fathers were born; and what was mere prophecy then has become commonplace now. God may be alive and well and living in Jacques Brel's apartment, but our contemporaries have experienced him more as an absence than as a presence.

With the crisis of faith there was bound to be a crisis of anthropology too, for our understanding of the nature of man had, until the present age at least, been tied completely to what we believed about God and creation. Taking our cue from the book of Genesis—and, more recently, from Calvin—we had always talked about the *imago dei*, the image of God. God had made man in his own image, and that formerly settled the most important questions about who and what man is. But without God, without creation by fiat, without the doctrine of *imago dei*, what is the image of man?

Thus the great tailspin of our times!

Some humanists in our century tried hard to hold the image of man where it was despite the loss of the transcendent. Hemingway, for instance, who talked a great deal about the vacuum God had left but tried to evoke the heroic in man by forever sending his leading men into precarious situations such as wars, bullfights, and hunting expeditions. And Heidegger, the philosopher, who seemed convinced that man's awareness of his own mortality made him somehow special and different from the animals. And Sartre and Camus, both of whom were members of the French Resistance movement and spoke of man's achieving authenticity and staving off nothingness by choosing the right actions in his life.

But the valiant effort was bound to fail. As Schubert Ogden has said in his book *The Reality of God*, there was something basically incompatible between the existentialists' humanism and their assumption that there is no God. Once they had swept theology aside, there was nothing left to prevent the ultimate erosion of their concept of humanity too.

We have seen that erosion—are seeing it now—in the writings and attitudes of the post-existentialist generation. The characters in Samuel Beckett's plays are dilapidated clowns and buffoons, enervated Charlie Chaplins, who are buffeted about the stage by strange and unseen forces, who long to die but haven't even the dignity or strength required to take their own lives. The same is true of the people in John Barth's novels. They cavort and frolic more wildly than Beckett's, but in the end they are overtaken by the same nihilism. The voices of both writers and critics today, says Richard Kostelanetz in *The New American Arts*, have merged to become one voice, and the message of that one voice is No! Thus has the positive passed into the negative, the yes-saying of Nietzsche into the no-saying of our own age.

Eugene Ionesco, one of the so-called dramatists of the absurd, has provided us with a powerful portrait of modern man in his play *Exit the King*. Bérenger, the king whose kingdom is crumbling before his very eyes, is a contemporary Everyman. Once he was strong and resourceful. He invented the wheelbarrow and the railway and the telephone. He built Rome, New York, Moscow, and Geneva. He wrote tragedies and comedies under the name of Shakespeare. He created revolutions and counter-revolutions, reform and counter-reform. But now he is powerless and all things are falling apart. The rivers are drying up, the soil is wearing out, the people are growing old, the census is declining, the Milky Way is curdling, snow is falling on the sun, the walls of the palace are collapsing—nothing will be left. "You've lost your power now," says the Queen, "over yourself and over the elements. You can't stop the rot and you've no more power over us." Even human relationships fail. One by one, the servants in the king's court disappear, just vanish into thin air, as he is no longer able to remember them. Even the old queen dematerializes. And finally the king himself, huddled in a blanket and bathed in an eerie gray light, is suddenly no longer there.

The play is a sobering, frightening experience—sobering because we recognize ourselves in it, frightening because we see the same thing happening to us and the world we live in.

We won't be healthy again, says Wladimir Weidlé, one of the most cultured and reliable voices in the world today, until we have made connection once more with the religious sources of our being. But how, having lost the connection, do we make it again? We recognize the ring of a certain truth in what he has said, but we no more know how to go about effecting a return to our religious roots than we know how to turn time backwards in its flight. We try! God—if there is a God—knows we try. But we just can't seem to make it.

Three major assumptions underlie the writing of this book. The first is that Weidlé is right, that it is imperative for us to recover a religious stance for existence, albeit one differing in many respects from the one judged lacking and discarded. The second is that there is a God and that *his* existence matters

profoundly in our daily affairs. The third is that, while the first
assumption may not be too great for many people, the second
doubtless is.

A word to those who cannot follow me in making the second
assumption is therefore in order.

It has seemed to me that the loss of our humanity affects the
state of our theology just as surely as the loss of our theology
affects the state of our humanity. That is, just as it is possible to
be too sick to accept love or too preoccupied to accept interest, it
is also possible to be too confused to accept belief in God—either
our belief or another's.

Take a case in point, the play by Ionesco to which I have
already alluded. At one place in the near-symphonic movement
of the play, there is a remarkable and very moving Litany to the
Dead in which all the characters implore the ghosts of the past,
the persons who have lived and died and become part of man's
history, to come to the aid of the expiring king. The old guard,
who is obviously very much devoted to his monarch, finally ends
the litany with the most desperate plea of all: "Oh you, great
Nothing, help the king!" It is apparent, from the author's capi-
talization of the word Nothing, that the historical void has been
apotheosized—has been turned into an empty divinity. And
therein is expressed the dilemma of the times. If man had not
lost his belief in God, his world would not be falling to ruin
around him; and if, on the other hand, his world were not lying
in ruins, he would probably believe in God and would not be
reduced to a vain and unreal dependence upon the "great Nothing."

There is bound to be a certain amount of reciprocity between
what we believe and how we are, and vice versa.

Suppose, then, that we attempted to achieve our human identity *as if* there were a God. Could it be that we would recover not
only our own human identity but, in the process, the experience
of God as well?

I do not intend to join here the arguments over the death of

[12]

God, either as Nietzsche meant it (and that passionate young man who vaulted the chancel rail at Notre Dame cathedral during an Easter service to shout from the altar, "God is dead!") or as the so-called (but self-styled) Radical Theologians mean it today, for arguing is nothing. God is, after all, inarguable. He either is or isn't, and we cannot say anything about him that is not in the final analysis only a reflection of our own experience, so that we have always ended by talking about ourselves and not about him.

But it is possible that we shall believe in God most heartily, in the very depths of our being, once we have rediscovered our zest for life by trying to restructure our humanity as though he did in fact exist and matter to us. The one may lead to the other.

It is to that end, to the recovery of our enthusiasm for being conscious, for being alive and alert from day to day, that this book is written. And it may be, if we succeed at all in this undertaking, that as part of our hidden agenda we shall recover God too—that as we become more real, so shall he!

I have believed for some time now, and become more and more convinced, that having the experience of God belongs to the category of serendipity—that is, among the things or truths or persons we discover only accidentally, without having intended to. Which is one trouble with being "religious"—thinking we have found God, or know where to find him, we stop looking for him in the places where he really is.

The phrase "finding God accidentally" describes nearly every great epoch in man's religious history.

But how does one go about finding something accidentally? There is a logical contradiction involved in the very way the question is put. Or is there? I remember the practical advice of a youngster whose parent had misplaced something and looked everywhere for it. "Go on and look for something else," he said; "it'll turn up."

Go on and look for something else. Maybe that's what we have to do—and wait for God to turn up.

[13]

Can it be that this is the church's true calling today, to be looking elsewhere while waiting for God to turn up? Possibly. When in the whole history of Christendom has there ever been an opportunity like ours for discovering so much about the nature of man, for turning a crisis in human identity into what the Japanese language, with no precise word for translating "crisis," calls a "dangerous opportunity"? And suppose that our understanding and respect for what is human are deepened and enriched by what we discover. Isn't it probable that we shall be in a new and advantageous position for discerning the presence and nature of God when these are disclosed to us?

This is no time to be forlorn about the absence of God, any more than a wife is forlorn when her husband is away on a trip. It is a time for reperceiving and growing, so that when he returns he will find us more exciting and attractive than when he left us. It is a time for reforming and reshaping ourselves. It is a time for rediscovering who we are and what our humanity really is.

Religion has unfortunately appeared in many instances to have had a baneful effect on people's humanity. But this is a time for correcting that. This is a time for being human again. And it may well be that the more we are human, and inhabit the earth, the more we will know the presence of God, and enter his Kingdom.

One final word: Many of the observations in this book—the more helpful ones—are not mine, but those of the many friends who have made life more real and exciting for me, and have thereby shared the presence of God with me. I cannot begin to name them all, but I shall not be surprised if they are able to recognize their contributions to what I have written.

The initial draft of the book was tried out first with a group of friends in the American Church in Paris, where I had the good fortune to be theologian-in-residence for the period of a year. Their constant enthusiasm in exploring the nature and dimensions of our common humanity inspired me not only as a teacher trying to find his way but as a person also trying to find his way. I have pondered whether the finished product of our discussions ought not really to be dedicated to them, rather than to my wife, to whom it owes first honor; but, knowing them as I do, they will gladly take this word in lieu of the honor and approve the dedication as an act of my humanity.

Chapter 1

Being Natural Before God

You HAVE PERHAPS NEVER THOUGHT of it quite this way, but it may be that the best thing you can ever do for God is to be yourself.

And that is a tall order.

Most of us have the idea that the *worst* thing we can do is to be ourselves, especially before God. We have acquired the notion somewhere that we cannot afford to be honest, to be who we are, and that we must always take care to project some other image, the one we think others—and God—would expect of us. We spend our lives hiding our real selves and putting forward our fabricated selves, our doctored alter-egos, our polite and respectable doubles.

Even those of us who boast of being "just what we are" and not concealing anything about ourselves recognize in moments of deeper insight that it is not really so, that there are levels of our personalities below which we have never dared to look,

[17]

where we are frightfully dishonest and secretive, veiling the truth even from ourselves.

The self we send out to meet God is almost always a false self.

The problem is that we think God expects a certain kind of behavior of us—a religious behavior. We imagine him as being straight and hard and intolerant, like a stern grandfather or a hanging judge. Our concept of him is all tangled up with what we know about religion and so-called religious people, which mostly has to do with a lot of restrictions and taboos.

We tend to think the way a Brazilian lad named Carlos did when he was being interviewed by writer Merle Miller about the approaching carnival season in Rio. They were standing in the warm sunshine looking up at the summit of the Corcovado, which is adorned by Paul Landowski's great white figure of Christ. "It will be sunny before Carnival and after," said Carlos; "but during Carnival it will rain, and clouds will cover the face of Christ. That is because He would not approve of what will go on."

"He would not approve." That is what we secretly think, what we unconsciously believe.

Therefore, we have developed a whole "religious" way of doing things, a false culture that stands over against the real culture, the true culture, that is real and true precisely because it is the one where we really want to live, where our flesh cries out to live, where our hearts are most at home. And we feel guilty when we do not subscribe to the false culture, particularly when we are at church or in those areas of our cultural life whose environs are most frequently described as holy. From the time that we were very young, we have been brought up to believe in this religious culture, and, as soon as we have children of our own, we begin to indoctrinate them into it also.

My wife recently came home with a clear example of this indoctrination process. She had overheard a church school teacher discussing prayer with the youngsters in her class. The teacher was trying to make the point that prayer can be thankfulness as well as petition. In concluding her lesson, she asked the children to name some things they were thankful for. One child said he was thankful for church and Sunday and music; another, for Jesus and kindness and friends; another for God himself. Finally one tow-headed little boy broke the pattern of responses by saying, with obviously perfect sincerity, that he was thankful for his dog and his bike. At this confession, the other children tittered and broke loose so gleefully that the teacher was compelled to scold them and restore order.

What was wrong with the information which the boy had volunteered? Nothing, really. He was possibly the most honest boy in the class. The others all recited the answers they had come to believe were *expected* of them in a religious environment. They were well on their way to the divorce between the sacred and secular orders of things that plagues most of our thinking about God and religion. If the same question had been asked somewhere else—on the playground or the post-office steps —their own replies would probably have been quite different.

One of the things that has made Holden Caulfield, the boy in J. D. Salinger's novel *The Catcher in the Rye,* a perennial favorite with the younger generation is his Huck Finn way of sizing up a situation and saying just what he thinks about it. There is no room in his philosophy for false ways of looking at things. I think my favorite passage in the novel is that one where Holden takes a girl friend to see the colorful Christmas extravaganza at Radio City Music Hall. Not for an instant is he taken in by the tinsel and the sentiment and the trumped-up religious symbolism, with men carrying crosses back and forth on the stage to the accompaniment of hymns and carols. "Good old Jesus," says Holden in his casual vernacular, . . . "would have puked at the sight!" "The thing Jesus *really* would've liked," he ventures with unerring judgment, "would be the guy that plays the kettle drums in the orchestra."

Blasphemers are so often right, because they are not taken in by the small pieties most of us fall prey to.

I remember an amusing tale from the days of one of my early pastorates, about the minister of a rural church nearby. It seems that the minister had arisen rather late on Sunday morning and was grouchily hurrying to get ready for church. As often happens when we are in the greatest haste, everything was going wrong. The minister was getting testier and testier. The climax came when his wife's cat, which he had always disliked rather intensely, scooted across the dresser top to avoid a swat he had aimed at it and sent his tie pin flying under the bed. Completely overcome with anger, the minister seized the cat and flung it against the wall, where it landed in a tight position behind a hot radiator and was greatly singed and disturbed before the minister's wife, hearing the sounds of torture, rushed to the room and rescued it.

Two hours later the minister, now composed and serene, the very soul of gentleness, was standing in the pulpit of his little church extolling the many virtues of Christian love. "When I am in Christ," he was saying, "I am possessed of great peace and calm, of a feeling of charity for everyone and everything." Whereupon his wife, who was sitting near the rear of the sanctuary and was possessed not of great peace and calm but of a near frenzy, said in such bitter audibility that nearly everyone on the back ten pews of the church was able to hear her, "Don't you believe him! Don't you believe him! The old hypocrite, you should see what he did to my cat!"

The polarities of our real and pretended existences are not usually this obvious, but they are there nevertheless.

One minister, Olov Hartman, was so disturbed a few years ago by the amount of sham he saw in people's religious professions that he wrote a novel which he called *Holy Masquerade*. The hero, or heroine, of the story was a minister's wife who finally went insane from watching her husband and his parishioners pretending, from a lack of courage and basic honesty, to be righteous and holy and whatever each of them thought the others expected him to be. The irony was that the minister's

wife, whom most people regarded as an impertinent noncon-
formist and even a hussy, because she was not wearing a mask as
they were, was in the end the truest Christian of them all.

We all wear masks, don't we? And paradoxically, when we
come together as the church, where we ought most freely to put
them off and be who we are, we are most prone to put them on
and be who we aren't.

"We strive continually," wrote Blaise Pascal, "to adorn and
preserve our imaginary self, neglecting the true one."

How right Pascal was! We spend all our energies on the
projected self and neglect the real one. We are always at pains
and expense to protect the image of the self that we have tried to
extend into the public mind, even though it may not be the
image that the public mind sees at all; and at the same time we
abandon and frustrate the self that is crying for recognition and
nurture, that is longing to come into its own and have an
existence it deserves in the world.

Isn't it true of all of us—especially in the church?

I recall with shame an occasion shortly after I had decided to
become a minister. Along with several other ministers, I was
participating in a prayer vigil for persons in our community who
were indifferent to spiritual concerns. The vigil had been arranged, by staggering the names of those who were to conduct
the prayers, to go on all night. Three or four of us, in our zeal for
the souls of the indifferent, had elected to remain throughout
the night, not retiring at all. As the night wore on, our prayers,
as I look back on them now, were inclined to become more and
more repetitious and sentimental. At one point they even became maudlin, and two of my friends actually fell upon the floor
in tears, begging God to kindle the desire for spiritual renewal in
the hearts of those who were the objects of our supplications. I
found myself ashamed of not having felt the same amount of
passion for these "benighted" persons that my companions felt.
Probably, had it been a normal hour and had our engagement in
prayer not been so arduous already, I should have continued

sitting there in an attitude of prayer, perhaps feeling a bit guilty all the while for not having reached the peak of devotion exhibited by my friends. But it was late and I was already overwhelmed by a sense of unreality. Before I knew what I was doing, I had collapsed to the floor beside the others and was weeping quite as loudly and convincingly as they. And I realized immediately, so that I have never forgotten it, that the only thing I was sincerely concerned about in that whole lachrymose setting was the opinion of my companions about me. I wanted them to think I was really religious!

This false moment, which I remember with such embarrassment now, is multiplied hundreds of times in each of our lives. We are so insecure in what we believe, so unlocated in the sea of behavior, and so practiced in our responses, that we find it difficult if not entirely impossible to react with honesty and candor to life around us. We have a way of acting, a way of hiding ourselves for the sake of our appearance before others, that finally confuses us. Like weary old actors who have spent their lives putting on the masks of all the parts they've played, we stand a little bit crazy at the center of the stage and try to figure out who we really are, what part is really ours, and whether we can play it at all when it comes down to that.

Wouldn't it be refreshing to God, and maybe to us too, if we just stopped the pretense and admitted how lost we are, how hard it is to be honest and natural, and how much we would really like to be ourselves before him?

One part of our lives where many of us find it extremely difficult to be natural and honest with God, because we are not at all sure what is natural and honest, is in the matter of everyday morality. We have heard the church say one thing and have seen the world around us doing another. If we are mainly of the world's opinion, as evidenced by our behavior, then how shall we represent this before God?

It is a vexing question. Unfortunately, many of us finally

evade the issue and don't bring it before God at all. We pull our masks a little tighter.

Take the matter of sex, for example.

We know now, at least since Freud, that life is unavoidably sexual or biological, although these terms must be taken at their full value and not as implying merely those things related directly to copulation or the so-called sexual acts. In other words, sexuality is largely involved in being natural; one is not really a natural creature until he has discovered a natural posture in relation to his sexual urges, ranging all the way from the ingestion of food and the defecation of waste material to an attitude toward his homosexual and heterosexual impulses.

Now, already a flag has gone down on the play for some readers. The mere mention of homosexual impulses is enough to cause some religious persons to withdraw and show signs of hostility. Yet psychologists insist that such impulses exist in every one of us, and some analysts even contend that every one of us passes through a period of homosexual love, either overtly or covertly, before beginning to relate to others heterosexually.

There isn't any hiding from the fact: we are sexual beings. Some are normally sexual, and some are abnormally so, but we are all sexual. Unfortunately, some of us are embarrassed about it in religious circles, for sex was long misunderstood and mistreated in those circles. But the fact remains that we are sexual to the core.

It is admittedly very difficult today to relate our innermost sexual feelings to God, because we had proceeded for centuries as though he were the archetypal Puritan father, perhaps the castrating father at that, and as though he expected us to be quite sexless despite the fact that the Bible credits him with having created both male and female and then left them naked in a garden. One would have thought that Nathaniel Hawthorne, the great New England novelist, had laid that lie to rest in his immortal story of *The Scarlet Letter,* which revealed that far more evil came from the church's attitude toward sins of the

[23]

flesh than from the sins themselves; or that Sinclair Lewis would have accomplished it with *Elmer Gantry,* his explosive novel about an extrovertish minister who delivered pious and dogmatic sermons from the pulpit of the same church building in whose basement rooms he lured choir girls and attractive parish wives, to their seduction. But the conflict between sex and religion is a habit of mind that is hard to overcome.

As a result of the long abuse and exploitation of sex by religion, we are now facing the over-compensating reaction of the *Playboy* philosophy, which tends to eventuate in sexual idolatry and an unabashed emphasis on the simplest and most direct gratification of the sexual urge with little sense of responsibility beyond the act, either to the other individual or to society in general. The position of Harvey Cox in *The Secular City,* that extraconjugal love is permissible but that it is a serious matter involving emotional and biological consequences which must not be taken lightly by either party, is a moderating one likely to commend itself to the modern Christian intelligence. And yet there remains among many people, despite the movement from Victorianism to an openness and candor in discussing sexual matters, an adamant unwillingness to grant that sex is a normal part of life, and, as such, a subject to be subsumed under the topic of Christian stewardship. Sex and guilt are still very closely associated in the mind of the average church member, and he blushes to admit in any kind of religious circle that he has even ordinary sexual ambitions.

It is not an easy thing, of course, to achieve naturalness in a matter whose roots of conflict are so deep in the subconscious. But the important thing is that we are beginning to understand that sex is not an area of life to be sealed off from our relationship to the transcendent, that it is, on the contrary, one of the great hidden forces in our lives that must somehow be brought before God for his blessing again. One of the things we so admired about Keith Miller's book *The Taste of New Wine* was the frankness with which he admitted the way his Christian pilgrimage was beset by physical temptations in the form of pretty secretaries and clients' wives. At least he openly identified the clash between his religious views and his natural urges, and didn't try to hide the natural man from the God he conceived along rather traditional Puritan lines. He did not spend his energies, as an author or as a person, trying to project an unreal image of himself; he understood that the God of grace is a God of grace precisely because he receives men for what they really are, not what they pretend to be.

This does not mean, of course, that we ought to abandon all previous moral attitudes toward sex and appropriate religion to sex the way the prostitute did who went out and purchased an oversized crucifix to hang over her bed. But it does mean that we ought more freely to explore our own minds and attitudes which have been darkly hidden even from our own consciousnesses, and to ask how the natural man with his immemorial urges is related to God. It may be that our artificialities and repressiveness have stunted not only our human relationships but our vision of life and God as well.

This was the concern of the English writer D. H. Lawrence, whose novel *Lady Chatterley's Lover* received such a scandalous reception when it was published in America a few years ago. Lawrence regarded the Puritanical spirit in sexual relationships, together with the advent of technology and the evils of capitalism and laissez-faire government, as a conspiracy to rob man of what is truly inimitable in him, his ability to love and enjoy the creation, to exult in blue skies and newborn chicks, to dance and frolic and laugh and sing. If he used four-letter words in his writing, it was not with the sense of prurience common to producers of pornography or even to small boys inscribing obscenities on rest room walls, but tenderly, beautifully, with a total appreciation for their Anglo-Saxon origins; artistically (and this may in the end be the real test for pornography) he imparted a richness to every word he used, redeeming it from foulness and unseemliness.

[25]

The phrase "an obscenity of false piety" comes to mind. How often our small moralities contribute to such an impression. A couple of years ago I was speaking to a conference of young people at a seminary campus on the west coast. I was trying to get them to see that we always tend to limit God by supposing there is an orthodoxy to love and grace, and forgetting that God has his secular side as well as his religious appearance. As an illustration, I cited a current novel in which a healthy heterosexual boy rejected an advance from a homosexual friend and then worried about whether he had done the right thing; suppose he had alienated the friend at a critical time in the friend's life. Was it possible, I queried, that here was a case of loving concern that God would understand even though we—society—didn't?

When I had finished speaking, the president of the seminary, motivated more I am sure by what some of his conservative trustees might say than by any suspicion of heterodoxy, stood and disclaimed any responsibility the seminary might have had in what was said; and the following week he began an aggressive campaign in his denominational circles to smear me as an "immoral" person—a campaign in which he was joined by the editor of the state denominational paper, even though that person had not been present and had never met me.

What is there in our makeup that persuades us that this kind of reaction is religious? Why don't we see that our pettier moralities are often the means of subverting true morality, of waylaying it and preventing its coming into its own? Do we really imagine that God must be defended and protected in such matters by our recriminations and caustic attacks? Don't we really suspect that we are posturing and being unnatural?

There are few estimates of Protestant moralism more scathing or more accurate than Langdon Gilkey's in *Shantung Compound,* a book of prison memoirs disclosing, among other things, the difference between the behavior of interned Catholic fathers and that of interned Protestant missionaries. The priests, he found, were accustomed to living in the world (paradoxically, for many of them had actually dwelled in monasteries), and related easily to men who swore, drank, gambled, and doped. The missionaries, on the other hand, tended to blanch before these signs of worldliness, and to retreat into the privacy of their religious shells.

Protestantism has produced, concludes Mr. Gilkey, "A degenerate moralism, a kind of legalism of life's petty vices that would be boring and pathetic did it not have such a terrible hold on so many hundreds of otherwise good-hearted people." It has resulted in a disastrous oversimplification of life, a blindness to ambiguities, so that those who hold it think that immortal life is consigned according to people's attitudes toward even minor moral vices. "I learned from this experience," says Mr. Gilkey, "that the fault in this Protestant ethic was not that these legalistic missionaries were too moral. Rather, it was that many of them were not free of their law to be moral enough. Their legalism prevented them from being as creative as the sincerity of their faith should have made them."

This was of course precisely the charge that St. Paul made against the excessive legalism of the Judaic religion in his day: it was so moralistic that it failed to be moral; it stumbled over small things and missed the big things. "Did you receive the Spirit by obeying the law," he asked the Christians in Galatia, "or by hearing the gospel?" Their legalistic attitudes had also begun to curb their creativity.

It is a personal kind of tragedy whenever anyone gets into this desiccating *cul-de-sac,* this unnerving deadend street that leads only to spiritual death and frustration and not to life and joy. I have a friend who was the minister of a very large church in a southern city. For several years he used his position of influence to lead a campaign against the legalization of the sale of liquor in that city. I have no doubt that he felt very heroic in the effort, for his life was threatened on more than one occasion; and he probably dreamed, at the same time, that he was serving God faithfully by his opposition to the liquor forces. After the cam-

[27]

paign was successfully over, and the people of the city had voted to ban the sale of intoxicating beverages, this friend accepted an invitation to teach for several years in a school in Europe. Imagine his shock, the first time he attended church in his new location, at being served communion with real wine! And then he learned that many of his colleagues, all of them professed Christians and many of them devout men, drank freely and openly in their homes and in restaurants. And one night he was taken to a room where one of Europe's most prominent theologians (certainly the one he had regarded most highly) was accustomed to talk casually with other professors and their students, and found that everyone in the room had a tankard of ale or a mug of beer in front of him, and that they apparently enjoyed their spirits as much as they did the conviviality of the theological exchange. Eventually the friend began to accept this as a normal way of life—he was too astute to mark it off as a wholesale defection from holiness—and finally he started sampling wines and liqueurs himself. When he returned to America a few years later, he was offered several extremely prominent pulpits. But reflection upon his earlier parish experience, which he now considered wasted years, had so disillusioned him with the Protestant ministry and the situation created for it by the expectancies of the laity of the church that he could not bear to consider such a position, and so accepted another kind of work.

How does one get out of the ghetto of too-small moralities, of legalistic trivia, and into the realm of the real, of the life-sized, of the truly significant? What does it mean to be natural before God? How does one find the creative middle way between legalism on one hand and libertinism on the other?

"The trouble with Christians," said a Buddhist friend of mine once, "is that they're not real." I have pondered that remark many times. Like all generalizations, of course, it is untrue. But all generalizations derive some truth from particular cases, and

there are certainly numerous particular cases where that assertion is accurate.

I have tended especially to remember the remark at times
when I have sat in church and looked around at the worshipers.
Some of them always seem to be going through an act, a performance, without any deep understanding of what is meant by
it but with only a compulsion to do what the others are doing, to
be respectable, to keep the mask on straight. They are like Mark
Twain's wife when she memorized a string of oaths and repeated
them to him in hopes it would make him stop cursing so much.
"You know the words, my dear," he laughed, "but you haven't
got the tune."

And then they go out into the world, still without the tune,
and lead crazy, mixed-up lives because their moral and spiritual
existence is only half-baked, because it is only on the surface,
like some horribly dried and fissured mudpack, and they are
constrained to wear it lest the rest of the world know who they
really are, lest they be caught walking the streets and riding the
subways in the pink-pearl shimmering powderedness of their
soul-nudity. Or maybe what they really fear is not to be seen by
the world, for there is that faint hint of exhibitionism deep inside
every one of us that even subconsciously at times exults in
betraying us by some deft act of indecent exposure, but to be
seen by themselves, to pass a glass or a mirror and to gasp in
horrified recognition at the sight of themselves as they are, *au
naturel* and mother-naked as the day they were born, only
worse, because there is an obscenity about old nakedness and
fat wrinkled flesh that there never was about flesh just born soft
and succulent and pinchable.

Why is it that we can't be real and Christian at the same
time? Is it because most of our so-called Christian responses are
learned responses, responses that aren't really natural to us at all?
Is that why there is such a division between what we pretend to
be (and sometimes think we really are) and what we really are

[29]

(only sometimes think we pretend to be)? We have all the rules for playing the game but we lack the motivation, we lack that inner impetus that would make us great players, that would in fact enable us to forget about rules and techniques and concentrate on the game itself.

This may sound like the so-called New Morality, but it is not really new at all. It is the same thing Jesus said when the lawyer thought to hang him up by inquiring of him as to which was the greatest commandment (isn't this debate an entertainment in every age?) and he replied, in effect, "Love God at the gut level and treat your neighbor the way you treat yourself." There wasn't much there the lawyer could argue about; Jesus had begun at the umbilical point where all rules must start if they are not, as appears to be the case with so much of our false morality, mere flotsam and jetsam from the wreck of some former system.

And Augustine, that sensualist turned saint and become the dual architect of both medieval and Reformation theology, said essentially the same thing, "Love God and do as you please." Not simply, "Do as you please," as the rule was with the Thélèmites, but "Love God," and then "do as you please." And that is of course the crux, the test, the point of separation between the new morality that is Christian and the new morality that is sub-Christian—or even anti-Christian—because it replaces God with an idolatry of the self, with hedonism and self-gratification, which are, when one considers that Augustine was also right in saying we are ever restless for God, finally, impossible solutions to anything.

It was this God-at-the-center business, this double-directed centrifugal-centripetal thing, this systole-diastole, contraction-expansion movement that gave Luther the confidence to say, "Sin bravely." We are going to sin. There is no use kidding ourselves about that, no use whitewashing the sordid truth. Man flies to sin as the sparks fly upward. What we would do, we do not, and what we would not do, we end up doing in spite of ourselves.

On our level, on the human level, things are that confused. Phariseeism and Puritanism are always fraught with a comedy of errors. Should we therefore slink through darkened alleys all our lives committing our transgressions behind garbage cans and in the shadows of second-stoop porches? No, says Luther; it is all out in the open now. Christ has died on that account. Now let us be manly in our sinning, bearing it like a slight infirmity and not like the heavy death it was formerly, before the Incarnation.

We must be careful where and how we quote Luther on this matter, I have come to understand. I talked once with a dear woman who was in great agony of soul because she wasn't sure she loved her husband. She had met him and married him when she was in the hospital and the doctors said she was going to die. But she hadn't died, and a dozen years later she had begun to wonder if she really did love the big, protective man she had wed. And he was so good to her, so tender and kind, that wondering made her feel guilty and remorseful. I almost laughed when she tearfully related the matter to me, and I would have had it not been so deadly serious to her. Of course she loved him—as perfectly or imperfectly as any of us loves his spouse of twelve or fifteen years. But she was confused by the romantic notions of love she had read about in boudoir magazines and witnessed enacted in the two-to-four slot on daily television. She was troubled because the only palpitations she was feeling were in her nervous system and not in her heart of hearts. And she imagined that God could not forgive her for her feelings, for that terrible apathy that just hung over her like a cloud from day to day. "I have tried to pray," she said, "but I can't. God can't hear me when I feel the way I do."

I tried to console her, to assure her that she wasn't the first person who had felt the way she did, and to remind her of some of the things I knew she understood about the nature of God. In my elatedness at learning that what troubled her was not really some deep, dark, and devious thing—I had expected much worse —I am sure I said a great many more things, and faster, than she could have comprehended. And one of the things I said, I hope parenthetically, though I am now by no means certain, was that Luther too had struggled with the problem of guilt and had finally concluded, after a great experience of grace, that we should "sin bravely."

Sometime afterwards, when the clouds had passed and the woman had learned again that she did indeed love her husband, a friend of hers was telling me about talking with her just after my conversation with her that tearful afternoon. The friend was laughing. "She was so puzzled," she said. "She just kept saying over and over, 'He told me to sin bravely.'" Of all the remarks I had made, she had seized upon that paradoxical one by Luther, and was apparently more disturbed than helped by it because she couldn't understand its meaning.

I am convinced, however, that it is a word we need to be reminded of again and again. Religion has taught us to be so rigid and unyielding with ourselves. We need to remember, those of us who are so unyielding, so "unco guid," as Robert Burns put it, that finitude is our element. We should not be in the habit of expecting too much of ourselves; the guilt and frustration we experience will only drive us to expect more and more, until we are sure to destroy ourselves in a spiralling, escalating race for righteousness.

To accept sinfulness as our natural state is not to abandon morality; on the contrary, it is to prepare the way for that deeper morality which issues from a sense of acceptance and gratitude. It is to appreciate creatureliness—and realize the meaning of grace.

Are we modern Christians students of psychology and yet keep our understanding of guilt and forgiveness separated into secular and sacred compartments? Have we thought for so long in terms of "sins"—of particular, isolated, discreet religious misdemeanors—that we are no longer able to consider sin as fallenness, as finitude, as a state of existence involving all of our problems as human beings? If that is so, then it must be awfully hard for us to reach any deep and meaningful level of forgiveness and self-acceptance.

Maybe this is why Franz Kafka is *the* novelist of the twentieth century—because he traced with such frightening clarity the paths of guilt and shame in the modern unconscious and made us face with fear and trembling the inscrutable contradictions of our moral existence. They were all there in his own life—the burdens of race and of nation, of affluence and of influence, of sex and of work—all crowding humanity to the wall and forcing it to defend itself until finally there was no defending itself any longer because he was tired, he was worn out, he was utterly depleted and defeated and accepted death at the hands of the tyrants who had invaded his life through his ancestors and his bloodstream where there was no getting at them to expel them, to expunge them, and be free before dying. Like Joseph K. in *The Trial*, who woke up on the morning of his thirty-third birthday and found himself under mysterious arrest for some unnameable crime which he was never to have specified for him, Kafka discovered that life is a narrowing co-existence with guilt, co-existence because it is there, intangible, ineluctable, ineradicable, and narrowing because it eventually squeezes a man out, restricts and constricts him until he can stand it no longer and gives up at last, ending not with a bang but a whimper. So he scribbled his novels and stories as attempts to hold on to his sanity; they were his emetic, his catharsis, his catheter for draining off the infection; and they have become the limpid, mirror-making pools in which we see the reflection of our own scared visages in the post-modern age, showing us the guilt and fever and self-doubt with which we are flushed almost beyond recognition of our selves.

For we have all drunk from the same well in our time, sucked poison at the same breast, and lost our innocence forever and a day. We don't know, since Freud, what we are responsible for and what we aren't. Life is an orange-colored confusion, and the despair or acidie we all experience at one time or another has underwritten time so that it has become the secret trustee of all our hopes and dreams. We cannot begin to decide which guilt is ours and which is not, and so we dismiss it all, which means in effect that we haven't dismissed any of it, but live under it as under a ledge, burrowing ever backwards and darkwards in our fear and apprehension.

"Repent!" scream the crudely lettered and anachronistic signboards along the macadamized jetways of our modern soul-journeys. Repent! And we are too tired, too shattered, too emptied of meaning to understand the meaning of that because we have not yet understood what it is to be absolved, to be accepted, to be forgiven, which is all necessary before one can begin to repent.

Shall we begin with the children? Growing up is the process by which innocence evaporates, isn't it? We often describe it as the transition from innocence to experience, and our literature and art abound with examples of the conversion.

An artist friend of mine has done a great series of canvases depicting the religious rites of the Doukhobars, that sect of Russian peasants which migrated several decades ago to the Canadian territory of Ottawa. He is fascinated by the "burnings," the occasions when the members of the sect set fire to their houses and barns, throw their clothing onto the blaze, and dance wildly about the flames in celebration of their "return to innocence." And in some of his paintings he has caught the real irony of the scene, with overfat, overbloated figures of lascivious-looking old peasants cavorting in the nude while wide-eyed, fully clothed little children stand around looking on in witless fascination at the sight. It is a dramatic inversion of innocence; and in the process of the ritual there occurs a kind of metampsychosis of the moral state, whereby the old people, trying to achieve innocence by their sympathetic magic, actually conduct the real innocents across the threshold into experience.

But isn't this the way of all flesh? Don't we all help, in one

[34]

way or another, to initiate the young into the sin of Adam, and to inculcate our confused values into the thinking of our children? And isn't their first real brush with guilt over the conflict between what we have taught them, maybe without meaning to, and what they feel instinctively, naturally, as a matter of course?

Someone has said, for example, that we teach children to lie at the same time that we are insisting that they always tell the truth. What we mean is that they mustn't fib to *us*. They mustn't tell falsehoods about their behavior or misrepresent conversations or exaggerate their status with their colleagues or understate the number of cookies they have taken from the cookie preserve. But on the other hand they must speak courteously to persons they do not like, reciprocate with thanks for gifts that arrived broken in the mail, and say "Yes, please" when passed the cauliflower or creamed spinach.

Or look at the teen-ager, that poor gangling creature, too old to be a child and too young to be an adult. In his demi-world of confusion and fear, he is beginning to long for relationships to persons and groups beyond the home. It is a natural yearning, part of the pattern of things at this time of life. But he has been taught patriotism and loyalty and gratitude, and he is hesitant about these new relationships because they seem to represent a betrayal of the family, an announcement that the family is not enough, is not adequate to his social needs. And if the parents are negative and unsympathetic and do not have some rudimentary understanding of the dynamic nature of the changes occurring in the child's sublife, they are prone to make matters worse by nagging the child, by berating or belittling his associates, by reminding him of his "obligations" to them and to the home, and by generally discouraging this inevitable thrust away from the nest. The child internalizes things, broods, sulks, picks at his food. More fussing. The resentment is driven deeper, and the guilt feelings grow larger.

Do we think that forgiveness and acceptance are realities

[35]

needed by adults, by men and women at life's great battleline? Then we do not know how that battleline is drawn and how it curves in upon the children.

And, of course, it becomes more and more complicated as we get older and the network of our associations becomes more varied and complex. A man begins to feel the problem of guilt especially when he has reached that barely definable point in his linear existence where he can see ahead and realize that he will never be much different from what he has already become, that he is the captive of his past and cannot transcend it, try as he will. Hope is no longer somewhere on the horizon. If he is to see it now, it must be in his children, his progeny, or else in the shabby, shuffling shape of cold reality, if he could only find it there. His job is no longer his dream; his future is no longer redemption; his wife is no longer the sweetheart of Sigma Chi. And he feels frustrated, defeated, humiliated, afraid. For he has been schooled to believe that everything is a man's own fault.

The wife, that retired and retiring old sweetheart of Sigma Chi, has problems enough of her own to cope with. For one thing, she was raised in a culture that has come to put its emphasis on youth and vitality, on the Ipana smile and the Ivory complexion and the Helene Curtiss coiffure, and she has never really learned to cope with the waning of loveliness, or to understand the forms it takes in its own successive transmutations. She rolls and creams and pants and paints and diets and dies—nearly —in the futile attempt to stave off wrinkles, overweight, varicose veins, blackheads, whiteheads, broken hair, gray hair, dull eyes, crusty cuticles, and a hundred other telltale marks of one's lengthening habitation in the world. And from time to time she weeps and sobs and gives it all up, eating gobs of whipped cream and chocolate cake and generally making like a poor man's Phyllis Diller, all out of the utter and unbearable hopelessness of it all. She dotes on her children and, when they refuse it, wonders if it isn't because she didn't dote on them enough at earlier and more critical times in their lives. She surprises her husband with affection and foolishness, and, when he retreats in bewilderment, thinks she has lost him and conjures up visions of his romping off to the woods with a bevy of Lolitas. Life has become a sullen, sodden lump of unhappiness and smothered desperation, and she knows she has failed, not grandly or gloriously, but miserably and certainly.

And for some people it never gets any better. There are more old people today than ever before, and what for? To feel helpless and weak and burdensome and dependent and humiliated and cranky and out of date and out of tune and out of pocket and out of zip? How many of the aged think of the end of life, for which Browning's Rabbi Ben Ezra said the first is made, as an impromptu collage of catheter tubes, social security checks, digestion pills, and back plasters! And the fact that they feel guilty about senescence is evidenced every time they apologize for being slow or for being out of breath after climbing the stairs or for not remembering some common thing, some familiar name out of their own past. They know better than anyone else the need for absolution and forgiveness, for they experience it sometimes like a pain in the groin, like an unbearable weight that is slowly driving them into the soft earth.

Guilt has many forms, but it is the basic situation of life, the one in which we all live, and the need for forgiveness is perhaps the greatest need we have in common. We long for total, absolute, complete and utter atonement. Most of us realize, when our defenses are down and we are shuddering under the need for forgiveness, that no half-way forgiveness will do us any good. Such a stop-gap measure would be almost worse than nothing at all; it would taunt us with its imperfection, with its limitation, adding failure to failure. What we want is an infinite and illimitable acceptance, as though the universe itself had undergone a spasm and shaken off the fever of our guilt, bringing life back to health and innocence; we want to be able to feel our forgiveness in the heart and along the blood, to know it is real and to know it is complete.

This is why "washed in the blood" religion is often so dramatically effective for people with an acute consciousness of guilt, and especially for people who can think and live mythologically, with huge and enviable simplicity, like children who really believe it when told that everything will be all right. They are fully warranted in discovering in the New Testament a full-blown doctrine of substitutionary atonement, with the crucified Christ as the perfect sacrifice, offered once and for all for the sins of the world, for the doctrine is there again and again, especially in Paul and John.

There was an ancient rite called the taurobolium, in which a man was put down in a pit and a bull was slaughtered over him, its great body supported by a grate while the blood from its jugular coursed down on the man all hot and bubbling and angry, and the man surely experienced a trauma unlike anything he had ever felt before, and dated his life from that sudden iron gate in the roadway of his memory. It is a little like that when a man becomes suddenly and violently aware of the death of Christ in his behalf, so that, in his mind's eye at least, the stigmata still flow with red liquid uncongealed by centuries of hanging there and the eyes still fix upon him with that pitiful motionless stare and he wants to cry and cry until he has sobbed out the last of his wretchedness and knows he has been cleansed of all his sin.

And there is a great deal of psychic unrest in people who cannot take their gospel this straight and simple and undiluted, who see problems, problems, problems—textual, psychological, philosophical, and are therefore only partially committed because they are only half-sure and still half-skeptical of their forgiveness. Like the colored auntie who loved her nip but thought it a sin, they have just enough religion to make them miserable and not enough to make them happy.

The sophistication which has almost become the myth of our time (our "coming of age," a theologian called it) has made it doubly hard for us to think singly, to believe that the isolated phenomenon of one man's death in first century Judea could really and truly be the answer to our complex psychological and sociological problems today. So we play at religion and retreat from any real involvement in it, from ever losing our heads or even our equilibrium and toppling into the lunacy of great religious passion. And we have developed a whole culture of subpriests known as psychiatrists and analysts and counselors to apply mustard plasters and salt baths to the migratory suppurating sores of our frustration and guiltiness that might have been purged more successfully if we had only been more simpleminded and could have believed.

But if Karl Menninger was right in that fascinating book *Man Against Himself,* we still try to pay for what we have taken from life; we still make our own little substitutionary atonements for sin. We don't always know that is what we're doing, but it is. We cut ourselves while shaving and slice our fingers with paring knives and fall down in familiar pathways, and many times we're exacting secret payment for some unconscious twinge of guilt. We drive too fast and work too hard and eat or drink too much as covert attempts at suicide, or murder of the self, usually because we have not measured up to our own strict code of morality, which we may not even know we had.

Does the nature of our tragedy begin to become apparent? We are unbelievably moral—even the libertines among us. And because we are moral, because we are equipped with this delicate seismograph that registers the smallest slips in our character, we feel guilty and need to find forgiveness. But the passing of the age of belief has left us marooned high and dry beyond the kind of absolution from sin men once experienced, and religion for many of us only serves to aggravate our problem by reminding us at regular intervals of the unfinished business that we have with our bad consciences. What do we do in the face of such a terrible dilemma?

For a beginning, why don't we simply make the plunge with God, and try to admit to him who we really are and what we really are down where we are full of fear and confusion and mixed-up emotions? It is not easy. As desperate as we are, we are still reluctant to turn ourselves inside out, like an old sweater, and reveal the hidden depths of our character; for, after all, we have not even seen them ourselves and how do we know we won't be shocked at what is revealed?

I remember a businessman telling me about the soul-confrontation fellowship to which he belonged—a kind of religious therapy group—and how excited he was about the insights he had had there into his own mind and heart. His voice was quite animated as he talked, and his eyes sparkled. "I get so scared," he said, "that one of these days that final mask will drop off and I'll be face to face with God."

I'm sure he didn't really expect it to go quite that far. He was too realistic a fellow not to know that he was speaking in hyperbole. But he was on the right track, wasn't he? We have lived too long as if there were a right side and a wrong side to religious confession, and as if a man daren't show anything but the right side to God. We have separated our secular natures and our sacred natures so long that we have got to believing in their being two different natures, and to thinking that God hasn't anything to do with the secular. Consequently, we have never exposed a vast part of our lives to his grace, or known in them the therapy of forgiveness and acceptance.

It is time we began to open those reserved areas and speak of them to God. It is amazing, when one does, how much he realizes he did not know about himself, how remote and hidden some of his drives and desires were from his conscious intelligence, where he had formerly gotten his only opinions of himself. Confession becomes an act of self-recognition, or discovery and reunification. And at the same time it restores humility, reminding the person of his dependence upon God and his place in a vast universe, so that he begins to hope again, and to be excited about the wonderment of life.

Paul Tournier, a Swiss medical doctor and counselor of international renown, has a remarkable sense of this wonderment. He is one of the most vivacious and effervescent men I have ever seen. He has spoken, in a little essay on *Fatigue and Modern Society,* of the first time he ever spent an hour waiting upon God in prayer and confession. He said he thought the hour would never pass. He set his watch upon the table, and from time to time he looked at it. When he guessed he had been praying for half an hour, it was only for a few moments. At the end of the hour, he had felt nothing. It had just been a test of his will power. He was the same as he had been in the beginning. But as he started to rise from his chair he felt a compulsion to stay a minute longer. And it was in that minute, he said, that God achieved the mastery of his life. The hour had been a necessary prelude. The minute had been the climax, and his life was never the same again.

Thereafter, he said, he found that this hour each day was the most important part of his life. He did not wish to face the affairs of the day without it. Often he would spend it laying out before God the things he was thinking about in his life, and the things he was planning to do. Sometimes, he said, God would tell him not to do those things, and would help him to keep his life simple and manageable and uncluttered.

What a wonderful effect all of this has had on Dr. Tournier's life! And would it really be any different for any person willing to undertake the discipline of confession and make it the vital center, the nerve center, of his whole existence? Not much, I am convinced; when I have tried it, it has worked.

That man with the fear of dropping his last mask and standing face to face with God—what do you think is really happening to him? Is it possible that he is getting closer and closer to his real identity, to the real him? Wouldn't it be wonderful if he finally found out who he really is, down under the veneers?

We're fearfully shy of the *I* now, and have been for some time. It has somehow become suspect in modern existence. Megalopolis, technopolis, Levittown, Organization Man, Lonely Crowd, the Bomb, Overkill, absurdity—all in conspiracy against the ego, the self, the irreducible, the final constituent, the one germinable grain in the bushels of chaff, the lone quavering voice under the deep well of echoes, lone ego-echo, the *I*, the *ich*, the *moi*. *I* has been taught not to raise its voice, not to trust itself, not to pit itself against the screaming, teeming (reaming?) mass; and if in the end it is cynical and does not believe in God, it may well be for the reason that it does not believe in itself.

What was it that the disarmingly charming middle-aged Puck of the Madison Avenue world, David Ogilvy, said quite frankly in *The Confessions of an Advertising Man,* that he will like us better if we are fond of roses and want to spend time with our children, but not to complain that we are not being promoted, because managers promote the men who produce the most? That is the key, isn't it? We are being geared to produce, not to *be.* The dimensions of mass require that we be fearful, hesitant, submissive, doubtful of our right to exist and to exert the old emotions of humanism. The machine is god. It is Juggernaut, and we are to cast ourselves under it in its ponderous forward moving. We are even taught that this is best for us, that being *au courant* is best, that being a cog in the great gearwheel of the future is best, that disappearing and abjuring our right to live and to dissent and to feel is best.

The church, so often in tandem with the great world's opinion and swung to and fro like the point-fixed and otherwise carefree tail of a puppydog, has not helped matters. For two or three generations now we have been hearing from both pulpit and lectern of the shamefulness of evangelistic hymnody and salvationist theology, whose primary error, we are instructed, is their emphasis on the individual and the personal aspects of redemption. "I come to the garden alone, while the dew is still on the roses," is privatistic, romanticized, saccharine—at least to a society that has stopped gardening and knows only cut roses from the hothouse. "What a Friend We Have in Jesus" is personalistic, falsified, and passé—at least in an age suspicious of friendship and dubious of the eternal lordship of Christ. How much better (we are told) to extol God as a mighty fortress (when ICBMs have shattered our trust in the most invincible shelters!) and to celebrate the fellowship of the saints as though it were a kind of endless sea where the identities of its multiple elements are faded and fused and lost (just when science has learned to distinguish among our various physical components like fingerprints, hair, and blood).

Certainly, the revivalistic tenor of our worship and preaching required challenging, if not on grounds of theology and psychology, then at least on grounds of taste and acceptability. But maybe, in a day of widespread anonymity and faceless congregations, it is time to tug at the other end of the rope, and to raise the issue of whether our hymns and manner of speaking have not become too impersonal, contributing to the rise of what Martin E. Marty has called "religion-in-general." Maybe it is time to face the terror and responsibility of the *I* again by standing it before God once more in its bonesome, lonesome selfhood and asking it to commit itself, to engage itself, one way or another.

What of the *I* and God? Do we ever manage otherwise to give a thing to God but generalities and new reports? Wasn't Kierkegaard right in seeing that real religion, religion that means something, begins at the point where individuals are compelled to pass through the narrowest of defiles, so that no two can march abreast, and to face the nameless benumbing terror of the Unknown who stands beyond? This was why he made it so hard on religion-in-general, why he threw brickbats at the organized church and hoary old tomatoes at reverend ministers and bishops, why he excoriated the church of his day until it reviled him and spat upon him and refused him burial in its sanctified and sanctimonious burial places. He said men would thank him for making it harder for them; and perhaps now we can understand the wisdom of what he meant. Until the *I* marches out alone into that foggy no-man's land, and stands there calling out to the mist till the echoes quit coming back and back, there is no relationship to God, and the death of God becomes a real plausibility, for the *I* is uncertain as hell of itself.

I confess that I too have joined the concert of voices against overmuch individualism in religion and have insisted at times on almost a coinherence among believers, a submergence of self in the corporate church, in the body of saints in all the ages. But I remember now with much pointedness that my own attachment to the church, that has since circumscribed my life, began in those bittersweet hours of late adolescence when I stopped by a gurgling brook or watched the moon in a fishpond or sat on a high hill looking at the world with God and thinking what I must do for him to make it all his again. I didn't live a day then without walking and talking with him (are the hymn lyrics so far-fetched?), without laughing and crying in the wind, without feeling like a young animal caught up in the rhythms of nature.

That was all very juvenile, of course, and I have since learned to curb the *I*, to muffle it and gag it and drug it and deter it and denature it until it is quite unsure of itself, sickened and humiliated and nearly destroyed. But not quite. It survives. And sometimes it revives. Sometimes it waxes again, and for a moment I feel something surging back, something like health or strength or power or excitement, something like life; and I wonder if I have not been wrong to hedge it and hurt it, to squelch it and welch on it, to bang it and bury it—if, maybe, it is not the better part of me, the only real part of me, the only real thing I have to give to the world or to God, the single, sole essence of what lives in my house and calls itself by my name. I wonder, in short, if I have not been guilty of murder, if I have not taken by suicide the life that God gave me to live and enjoy in the world.

Now I am wicked, for I have decided to indulge the *I*. I am tired of being submerged in the mass, for I never felt a real identity in the mass. I thirst to feel again, and to feel until my body aches and throbs with the sensation, until the sensation masters me and overcomes me. I have decided that sinning bravely entails being who I am, accepting my limitations, endorsing them, *capitalizing* on them. I can live no longer in that state of suspended animation where one always waits for the next report to come in, for the next scientific discovery or the next theory of aesthetics or the next Dead Sea scroll. Life is now and it is personal and it is individual and it is cock-eyed and it is wild and it is unpredictable and it is insusceptible of categorization and I must live it as it comes, live it with every possibility of error, live it with every limitation looking on, or I lose it, flatly and definitively, without ever a chance to have it back again.

How important it is to affirm this *I;* how important not to overleap it to get to the general, the universal, the "acceptable."

Man's true work does not begin until he understands what is inimitable about his way of doing it and thus repeats and extends himself in his produce; his true marriage does not occur until he sees it as an opportunity for sharing and enjoying the differences between two persons, each of whom contributes his most unique self to the bargain. Man's true religion does not come about until he regards it as the offering of his most inner self, or his idiosyncrasies and peculiarities as well as his more common virtues, to the God who has revealed himself supremely as a person and as one with peculiarities of his own.

I saw a girl in an art class once painting a picture of a young woman and flowers. This particular girl seemed always to work in delicate shades of pastels, and the picture was quite pleasant to look upon. Another canvas, a much larger one, sat nearby as she worked. The colors were similar, but the forms were very different. It was an abstract painting, and, although there were flowers recognizable in it too, it had a wildness about it that was not in the smaller painting. When the art instructor came to her easel to watch her at work, I thought he would praise the new painting for its obvious loveliness. But he didn't. He studied it a moment, and then he said, "Why did you change from your earlier style? This doesn't look like you at all." The girl was not at all embarrassed by the reproach. "It's a present for my grandmother," she said, "and I know she wouldn't care for something

[45]

abstract. This looks like my grandmother." "Ah," said the instructor, "that is the reason. But I think you are underestimating your grandmother. She doesn't just want a painting, she wants *you*. And you are in the other painting."

As I studied the two pictures after that, I realized that what the instructor said was true. I could see the girl's personality in the larger painting more than in the smaller one. And the artistry of the second began to seem contrived, cribbed, and narrow.

Rabindranath Tagore, the Hindu philosopher and poet, recorded a similar observation in his book *The Religion of Man*. He recalled his childhood and the simple, handmade toys he and his friends were accustomed to play with. One day a boy entered the group with a manufactured toy. It had no rough edges. It gleamed with several coats of paint. All the other children envied the boy for having it. But Tagore remembered years later the tragic sense he felt on seeing the toy: it had none of the boy's personality in it. Because the boy had not made it, it remained a thing apart. It was not an extension of his life. It lacked what Tagore calls the *dharma*, or virtue, of the person.

It is difficult in a technocratic society to keep in touch with one's own *dharma*. And yet we must, for in the end it is the only thing that prevents our insanity, our loss of a point of reference, our loss of nerve. We must even pray to be ourselves, to know who we are and how to excel at being ourselves.

But, it is interposed, isn't this preoccupation with the self a form of sin? Isn't it the Narcissism, the pride, the *hubris*, that Augustine once defined as the classical sin? Is it not diametrically opposed to the Christian view of things, that would make God the center of gravity with all things converging upon him?

Perhaps it is. This may be part of the net we are snared in. We are finite, and our best efforts to worship the infinite eventually run afoul and return upon us. Freud was quite right: God is a projection of our own desire for a super parent. (He was likewise wrong, for God is also more than this.) But there is no other way for us. In the end we can only hope to give him our selves; and to do that, we must first define the self, must recognize it and delight in it and even love it. Yes, *love* it.

It was Bernard of Clairvaux, the great mystic and administrator of monasteries, who proposed a "ladder of love" for the soul's glad pilgrimage. It explains better than anything I have ever seen how important it is that a man love himself and not despise himself, as we are so wont to do. On the first step of the ladder, said Bernard, we love self for self's sake. This is the wide step where most of humanity lives and remains, never aspiring to more. It accounts for the undisciplined selfishness which abounds in the world. But there is a second step, where men love God for self's sake. This is the general world of religion where men love God acquisitively for what it does for them. It, too, is a wide step, for there are many men who never go beyond it. For some men who aspire to go on, however, there is a third step where we love God for God's sake. It is a very difficult step to take, and there are far fewer persons who ever manage it. How does one begin to get inside the mind of God and to love him for his own sake? Yet, incredible as it seems, there is a step of devotion even beyond this one, a fourth step reached by only a few persons, where men have learned to love self for God's sake.

Love self for self's sake
Love God for self's sake
Love God for God's sake
Love self for God's sake

There is the paradox, that a man can actually love himself for the sake of God, can give glory to the Creator of all things by living gloriously, can love the Creator by loving life, can worship the Creator by appreciating himself. What else did the writer of the eighth psalm intend by the rhetorical exclamation, "What is man, that thou art mindful of him, and the son of man, that thou visiteth him?" Man exults in God most truly when he is able to exult in his own creatureliness, in his own human nature, in his own mortal gifts.

Chapter 2

Keeping the Sense of Wonder Alive

GOD DOES NOT DIE on the day when we cease to believe in a personal deity," wrote Dag Hammarskjöld, "but we die on the day when our lives cease to be illumined by the steady radiance, renewed daily, of a wonder, the source of which is beyond all reason."

How true!

When was the last time you were really excited about something? Do you remember? Is a man really most alive when he is most full of wonder and excitement? Is he most a person then? If he is, then why do we spend so little time concentrating on the mystery and fascination of the world around us?

I read once about a man who always cut his books (European books in the days when publishers did not separate the pages) *upside down* so that he didn't absorb too much of the contents as he worked, and about another man who had to stop going to High Mass because the beauty of it excited him until he was overwrought.

[48]

What a world we live in! And yet some of us are so intent on our jobs or our education or our daily routines that we miss the magic and speak of how dull or boring life is. It is a pity.

Recently, I talked with a man who was an executive in a grocery chain operation. Expansions in the company had opened many vacancies in the upper echelons of its management, and he had been tapped for a significant promotion. But he was beginning to be afraid of his own desire to work: was it gradually starving out everything else in his life? Already his wife and children were complaining that they did not see enough of him. Suppose he took the promotion. It would mean even longer and harder hours, even more time away from home. Would he be committing himself to a program from which he could never again be extricated until it was too late to enjoy his youth and his wife and his children? Would he awaken some day to the fact that he had missed out on life, had just let it go by because he was too busy with his job? Was he forfeiting the beauty and wonder of life by being so active that he had no time actually to contemplate it?

"Do any human beings ever realize life while they live it?" asks Emily in Thornton Wilder's *Our Town;* "—every, every minute?" "No," says the Stage Manager. Then, after a pause, he adds: "The saints and poets, maybe—they do some."

The saints and the poets. The saints, who are devoted to the Creator, and the poets (or artists), who are devoted to the creation.

Is it possible, in Protestantism, that we have had an overdose of saintliness and not enough poetry? That we have developed a kind of spiritual docetism because we have not associated God and his world as we should have? In the Bible, especially in the early chapters of Genesis, in Psalms, and in the New Testament, there is a strong correlation between the simple awareness of creation as the creator's and the sense of worship. Man sees the world he lives in, is filled with awe at its intricacy and variety, and adores the mysterious hand that shaped it all. The animals, trees, starlit nights, all compel in him a feeling for transcendence, for the otherness informing and going beyond what is seen and touched and heard. They instill in him the sense of the holy, of the *mysterium tremendum,* of angels ascending and descending between two realms. The world shares the wonder of God, because he made it. It expresses the wildness, the depth, the infinite variety of his being. Therefore the world humbles a man and instills in him a feeling of worship and reverence.

The saints and poets. For the poet realizes life while he lives it, and he helps us to realize it too.

Picasso understands this as his mission in painting—he distorts everything in order to make us see it better. And Christopher Fry, the playwright, defines poetry and drama the same way: its business is to make us suddenly aware of what we have known from the beginning but have simply failed to realize. This is the way art redeems us from dullness and dreariness, from the death of the eye. It stands us on our heads to see what we had been seeing all along but never noticed. A poem like George Starbuck's "Visit to a Museum" or a painting by Brueghel or a prose description like that one of the winter morning in John Updike's *The Centaur* awakens us to the piquancy and the vibrancy of the life around us, to the mad, wonderful welter of waifs and wisteria, comets and tadpoles, gravel and grandeur surrounding us every hour that we live.

It is hardly to be wondered at that one California university has begun to offer what is known in the curriculum as sensitivity courses, with scores of young people standing on a breeze-swept hilltop overlooking a Pacific sound and imagining that they are the wind in the grass, or its sound in the trees, or the noise of the surf. We have become so dead to feeling, so inured to wonder. The stimuli of our age have been so gross as almost to kill off the senses, or at least to dampen and mute them. Television, radio, rock-and-roll, jet planes, sonic booms, housing projects, concrete jungles, land erosion, water pollution, traffic congestion, smog, saturation advertising, 30,000 new book titles a year: we are the first generation in the history of mankind to commit suicide by orgy!

Is it any wonder that we are talking about the death of God? That is about all we're up to believing in, isn't it? Our malaise is so general, so widespread, that we don't even recognize it for what it is. We don't realize that wonder has disappeared from our existence, that we don't get lumps in our throats any more, or shivers up the spine, and that when we talk about anything so preposterous as the death of God, what we are really saying is that something has died inside of us, in man, in the human heart.

I remember when I was a college student and was not so well off as I have generally been since. One year I could afford only two meals a day—a bit of breakfast and then a simple but nourishing supper. I remember how wonderful food seemed to me that year. A glass of milk was a friend. A pork chop was a feast. An orange was a miracle. Occasionally, my fiancée would mail me a little box of cookies. They usually arrived broken and crumbled. But they were a treat beyond description to me. I was very hard on myself about eating them and would allow myself just a couple a day. Sometimes I would open the drawer where I kept them and take out the box just to smell them. And when there was nothing left in the box but the crumbs, they were given their due of importance and ceremony too; knowing they were the end of the supply, I would eat them carefully so as to savor their taste as fully and as long as possible.

The year after that my wife and I were married. She had just graduated from high school and I had not finished college yet. With a hundred dollars in our pockets and an old car full of our belongings, we set out to go twelve hundred miles from home to the school where I would complete my work for a degree. By the time we got there we didn't even have enough money to pay the first term's tuition. We both worked at odd jobs all through the year to get by. We budgeted a dollar a day for our food and never bought more than a dollar's worth of gasoline for the car. At Christmas time, we bought each other a few little presents that were quite necessary. I don't think my wife has ever had anything she was prouder of than a mop she received. Frequently, on Sunday afternoons we would go to the park and walk past the vendor selling snow cones. They cost a nickel apiece and came in several flavors. We would decide if we really wanted one badly enough to spend the money for it. When we did, we would get one—and share it.

The funny thing is, life has never been more beautiful for us than it was right then. The sky never looked bluer, the frost sparklier, the stars brighter. Food has never tasted better. Christmas has never seemed bigger or more meaningful. My wife bought three new dresses that year for eleven dollars. Now she buys garments that cost many times that much. But she has never had a dress of which she was prouder than she was of those simple cotton garments purchased in a cut rate shop.

Is it possible that many of us have too much now to be happy? Can a person be so well off that it's not really good for him? That he forgets what it is to be alive in the universe? Gabriel Marcel said once in a book called *Being and Having* that when a man begins to have too much it affects his ability to *be* anything. His possessions begin to possess him. He ceases to be aware of the mystery of life around him. Life becomes tedious and tiresome.

Do you remember Diogenes who gave away everything he had except a shard of old pottery which he retained to use as a drinking vessel? Then one day he saw a small boy cupping his hands to drink from a fountain, and he threw the shard away. Is there a freedom in the lack of possessions? Does it make us more sensitive to the world around us?

The answer is not unqualified. It depends on the person. Some people cannot stand to be poor. It makes them envious and bitter. They are always in an ill temper because somebody else has something that they want and cannot afford to have. Some people cannot live happily with wealth. It becomes an obsession to them. They worry lest they will lose it. They worry lest they are not enjoying it fully. They grieve about taxation. They are afraid that people like them only for what they have, not for who they are. They know their relatives will squabble over the property when they die.

In general, though, it is correct to say that possessions can distract us from the priceless wonder of life around us. They can help to make life so secure and antiseptic that we cease to be excited any more. And that is a shame. It is tragic for any person to be so anesthetized to his surroundings that he is able to live for days at a time without noticing the beauty of old pewter or the smell of new bread or the magic of a frost-covered window pane. Life is the most precious gift we have, and there is something dreadfully wrong with us when we let it slip by without even being mindful of it. It is better to suffer, and be conscious, than to exist in euphoria and not be aware of things.

"Give us our daily bread," says the great prayer of Jesus. There is something very wise in that. Stockpiles and surpluses do not help to engender the spirit of delight in us. But daily bread—that is an act, a miracle, a gift, something for which to be grateful. We can comprehend it, encompass it, receive it. It feeds the person without enslaving him, without burdening him, without drugging him. It reminds him of what he is—and *whose*.

Whence arose the idea that a man can have plenty and still be a godly man? Oddly enough, it is a biblical idea. The ancient Hebrews were a very this-worldly people, and they figured that God rewarded faithful men in terms of the world's goods. Abraham was a rich man because he was the father of the chosen people. But Jesus, though a Hebrew, saw the danger in having great possessions. Like the Rich Fool in his parable, we begin to think that *we* have made the wealth we enjoy; we lose the sense of dependency, and then the world shrinks up to the size of our own breadbaskets. It is easier for a camel, that big lumbering beast on stilts, with all kinds of baggage tied on him akimbo, to scrape through the narrow little gate in Jerusalem known as the Needle's Eye than it is for a rich man, with all of *his* baggage, to get into heaven. Jesus didn't say it is impossible for a rich man to be godly; he just noted how extremely difficult it is.

How dreadful for the affluent society! How awful for the big spenders, the waste-makers, the over-consumers! How terrible for men and women who live in a nylon and plastic society, with thermostatically controlled heat and air conditioning, and rheostatically controlled lighting, and electronic air filters and dehumidifiers, and electric freezers and electric ranges and electric typewriters and automatic garage doors and steam-heated driveways! How will we ever remember God? What need do we have of him?

And there is the catch! The comforts of our life today betray us into supposing life is a little more neat and orderly than it really is. In a society where one never gets so cold that his bones burn like dry ice inside him, or so hungry that the sight of food nauseates him, or so lost that he figures to starve before finding his way back, or so full of pain that he is afraid he *won't* die, we are quickly deceived into believing ourselves the masters of our fate, the sole and unconditional architects of our own happiness and satisfaction. Our dependence (we think) is no longer on the sun and the rain, the wind and the frost, the stream and the field; it is no longer on nature and no longer on God; it is on maintenance crews and traffic conditions and the national economy and international politics. We are part of an incredibly complicated and interdependent social network, and our greatest problem is *conditioning*—all men must be conditioned to accept their place in the wobbling, unsteady whole, and not to push too far or too suddenly in any new direction lest they unwittingly destroy the equilibrium of the whole and bring it to utter chaos. Then man would be fallen again. Then we would lose our paradise.

Is there a way to worship God in the modern world? Perhaps. We may be able to help our children find the way, even though

[54]

it is hard for us. Suppose we begin to teach them that the real frontiers in life, those borderlines of experience where man's control breaks down and grace takes over, have always been inner things and not outer; that, even in an age when man is unleashing nuclear power and designing megalopoli with total weather and air control, there are deeps within man that have not and probably will never be plumbed; and that these mysterious and bottomless recesses are really the places where man has always met God, where he has always striven with the Dark Stranger, where he has always discovered the real communion with what is beyond him.

And maybe our children, growing up accustomed to the new world that has only sprung on the rest of us overnight, as it were, will know a sense of wonder that goes beyond our amazement at discrete and disparate marvels of the times and sees the infinite and unifying spirit on which this age is just as dependent as the ones before it.

Meanwhile, we are the experienced ones, the old ones, the tired ones. We are the ones who have lost the sense of wonder.

How do we go about recovering the sense of wonder? Suppose we realize that something in us has died, that we are no longer really aware of life around us. What can we do to regain our awareness?

It may help to slow down, to cut the pace of things, to idle our motors and turn our sensitivity volume up. If part of our trouble is that we live too fast and have too much, we may improve the situation by purposely simplifying our existence.

This was what Thoreau, that remarkably modern man who lived in the nineteenth century, recommended. He said that he had reckoned what were the four basic ingredients to keeping alive in his day and in his part of the world—food, fuel, shelter, and clothing—and that most people had no idea how easily one could get along on a little of each. He had no truck with what John Ruskin once called "the goddess of getting on." He figured

[55]

that we start out just about as far ahead as we'll ever get, and that all the frantic activity to get any further just lands us farther behind. He said that he had found it true in his own life that in proportion as one reduces the complexity of his existence he discovers the universe around him to be friendly and well-intentioned.

This is just as true for us today as it was for Thoreau a hundred years ago, isn't it? Many of us seem to be bent upon self-destruction, paradoxically, by success: we give ourselves so much, and engage in such a whirl of activities, that we lose sight of the things that really give meaning and purpose to life. As William Faulkner wrote in one of his novels, life begins to go so fast that accepting takes the place of knowing and believing. We no longer remember who we are, or what our personhood is, or how we are related to the universe around us. But if we go the other way, and reduce the complications, we begin to be healthy again. We discern what we are really like, and what the world is like. We become centers of meaning. When we stop rushing our sensations, they become clear and strong again, and we feel revitalized.

There is an illustration of how this works in Viktor Frankl's classic little book *Man's Search for Meaning*, which consists of psychiatrist Frankl's memories and observations of life in a Nazi prison camp. Frankl said that as the inner life of a prisoner became more isolated and intense, he experienced the beauty of art and nature as never before in his life. Somehow deprivation made the eye more observant, the ear more attentive. One evening when Frankl was in a Bavarian camp, a prisoner came running into the building where the others were all huddled on the floor, resting and eating their ration of soup, and cried for them to rush out into the assembly ground and see the beautiful sunset. Tired as they were, they went out, and stood in hushed admiration before the brilliant hues of the evening sky, running all the way from fiery red to steel blue. The sky, mirrored in every small puddle of water standing on the ground, was a dazzling contrast to the drabness of the gray mud huts of the camp. After several minutes of deep silence, one prisoner remarked, "How beautiful the world *could* be!"

These are exaggerated circumstances, and ones in which we may all wish never to find ourselves; but the manner in which physical deprivation makes the appreciation of the world more acute applies to all of us. As the pressures on our field of awareness are reduced, our minds and nervous systems begin to unscramble and interpret more clearly the data they receive. Life begins to assume its real proportions of grandeur and majesty.

Maybe it is important for us to be always on the lookout for *new* wonder. We tend to identify it too exclusively with the things that have stirred us and moved us before, and, because things cannot be the way they once were, we live with nostalgia instead of excitement. We remember the trees in the apple orchard of our youth and the fun we had in college and the moonlit nights when we were on vacation in Trinidad. But what of the trees on our street now and the fun of being alive now and the moonscapes at home? What of the millions of things crowding around us now with their beauty and piquancy and delight? Aren't there new sights, new sounds, new tastes to stimulate our responses? Why must all the good things be in the past?

I used to live in the past a great deal. Certain images, ideals, insights, decisions, of my youth had become fixations for me. I lived by recreating them in the present, by bending every situation around until it constituted a repeat performance of what had already been. Then one day I realized how I was sinning against the present. The present was just as rich as the past had been when it was the present; only I was missing life in the present because I could not get over my monumental attachment to the past. Slowly I began to understand how to relate to the present again, how to enjoy its experiences with the same zest that had led me to enshrine the experiences of the past, yet without enshrining those of the present. It dawned on me then that life is full of wonderful encounters from the beginning all the way to the end, if only we don't get hung up along the path. I began to see that the open-endedness of human existence is one of its most remarkable qualities. That we *don't* know what is coming around the corner, that we *don't* have any rules for handling novel experiences, is part of the sheer richness of our lives. It is in constant encounter with the new that we are constantly reborn. The opportunity for creativity lies precisely in the realm of what we have not experienced before. We are molded as persons as we give shape to the ever-changing data of reality around us.

Many people are like the old professor in Ingmar Bergman's film *Wild Strawberries*, who dreamed one night he was taking an early morning walk in the empty streets of his town when a funeral procession turned into the churchyard just ahead of him. Just as the wagon bearing the coffin made the sharp turn to enter the churchyard, a wheel wrenched loose and the coffin rolled off at his feet, dislodging the corpse. Left alone in the street with the body, the professor reluctantly took hold of it to put it back in its box. But a strange thing happened: the corpse seized his arm and struggled with him until they stood face to face! In horror, the professor regarded the visage of the dead man. It was his own! When he woke from the dream, the professor realized its meaning at once. He had been living as a dead man. His thinking, his appetites, his personal attachments, were all fixed somewhere in the past. He was a living, walking corpse. It was a terrible vision, but, in effect, it saved his life. He would not get into that condition again.

This is essentially the effect the existentialists have tried to induce repeatedly in human existence by their insistence on facing-death situations, on what Martin Heidegger has termed our "running forward toward death." Man is the only animal who lives with an awareness of his own end, of his own ceasing to be; and he achieves his manhood more easily, therefore, by contemplating his future annihilation and living his life fully until it comes. The existentialist writer is always making characters look down from bridges or precipices or tall buildings and remember what life is about, or look into the muzzle of a gun and realize what existence is when denuded of all the encumbrances we are wont to put upon it in modern society.

Most of us have experienced the same sort of thing in times of serious illness. Life is then interrupted from its steady onward flow. The possibility of death becomes real. We suddenly realize what things in life are important and what things are not. Often the result is a whole new scale of values, with things that were previously very significant to us sometimes reduced almost to the point of invisibility, while things to which we had paid little attention assume positions of great importance.

And what wonderful times the days of recovery are! The world comes winging in upon us at a thousand angles, rushing us with sensations too rich and varied for cataloguing. All our impressions are fresh, sharp, distinct. The leaves on the trees are clearer and lovelier, more intricate and more multitudinous. The sky is bluer, stronger, more alive. The movement of life around us is more vivid and exciting. Life is seeing, life is feeling, life is being aware, life is breathing, life is exulting, life is being alive, and being alive is being receptive.

But a man ought not to have to get into a hard place, into a confrontation with death itself, in order to experience the world like this, ought he? A man ought to remember that he is mortal, that, in one sense, he walks the world as a stranger, and so keep himself sharp and receptive to the impressions life would always be making on him. He ought to wait and listen a great deal, as a guest, and so receive more and more of what the world has for him.

That rich man in Jesus' parable—the one with the over-laden barns—he had forgotten that death stalked him, hadn't he? And he had therefore lost his sense of dependence and thought the world depended on him. Nothing is marvelous to a man who has lost the feeling of dependency, except maybe himself, and that is small marvel. But how ineffably rich the world is to the man who knows he is dependent, that he waits upon the world, and, so waiting, upon God.

Maybe this is the special condition of childhood, and of its feeling for the miraculous. The child knows he is dependent. He may rebel against those on whom he depends, and yet revel in the very sense of dependency. It is his special security, to be dependent. And something happens the minute we begin to think we are no longer dependent, that we are free and unfettered and—responsible. We begin to be tense and to worry. How will we ever fulfill our obligations? How will we manage to acquit ourselves? How will we become successful? And the magic begins to die. We say it is facing reality. But what is reality? Is it our dull and colorless view of things when we have forgotten the joy and ecstasy of childhood?

Again I draw on personal experience. No one ever felt more independent than I did as a youth. I was clever enough to get on in life, I enjoyed inordinately good health, and I had been essentially making my own way in the world since I was fourteen or fifteen years old. I went from success to success. A friend of mine said once that I had the Midas Touch, and that, figuratively speaking, everything my hand fell on turned to gold. Consequently, I had the idea that I could do pretty well what I wanted to in life; I thought there were no doors that could not be opened by either strength or resourcefulness. And my religion only reinforced this notion, for I believed that personal righteousness would supply whatever was lacking in either of these other characteristics.

But life dried up for me as I lived by this philosophy. I didn't realize it at the time, but the world was getting smaller and tighter and more highly organized for me. And then one day, maybe the same day when I stopped living in the past, I saw that my independence of everything was false, that it didn't really exist at all. It only seemed to be independence because I had cut the universe down to my size. It was a tragic inversion: I had increased and the world and God had decreased.

The way back from such a situation is fortunately much quicker than the way into it. Once a man sees what has happened to him and how he has become the demi-monarch of a world of his own making, that world is shattered and his crown is forfeited. He despises himself for what he has done, for how he has let life get caught up in a corner. I did. I literally condemned myself. I didn't know how I could have been so stupid. But my self-berating was actually a survival of my old attitude: if I could not be the king of one territory, I would scold myself for having lost another. Eventually, I realized that a proper view of the world will help a man to accept even his own weaknesses and mistakes and that self-contempt is an unworthy attitude in the face of life's wideness and variety.

Now I understand something of the joy of living appreciatively, with a feeling of dependence on the world and others and God. Some of the most beautiful moments I have are the ones when things have gone wrong and I am left alone in my brokenness to contemplate the ruins. The ruins, yes, because this frequently comes of my efforts to be a man in the world. Beautiful, yes again, because over the very ruins of my own efforts I remember the sovereignty of God and the glory of being alive.

I spoke of the dependency of childhood. Sometimes it helps to recover the sense of wonder if we just try to see the world through a child's eyes. Not long ago I was busily at work at my desk when one of my sons came bounding into the room with a freshly-made drawing in his hand. My first impulse, because I was so engrossed in what I was doing, was to send him scuttling into another part of the house, as I am all too frequently guilty of doing. But something inside me dissuaded me from doing this, and I took him up in my lap and looked at what he had drawn and colored. "How important this is in his eyes!" I thought. "How vivid the roughly applied colors must appear to his young

[61]

mind! I will try to look at it as if I were he. I will see it through
his eyes." And for days afterwards that child's vision remained in
my head—the richness of the colors, the importance of the
imprecise forms, the total excitement of the experience. For a
while, at least, it reminded me that life is far richer when we
don't try to impose our own order, our own sense of value, on it
without waiting first to see if it has one of its own.

Perhaps this is why Michel Quoist has written, in *Prayers of
Life,*

> God says: I like youngsters. I want people to be like them.
> I don't like old people unless they are still children.
> I want only children in my kingdom; this has been decreed from
> the beginning of time.
> Youngsters—twisted, humped, wrinkled, white-bearded—all kinds
> of youngsters, but youngsters.
> There is no changing it, it has been decided, there is room for no
> one else.
> I like little children because my likeness has not yet been dulled
> in them.[1]

What is the likeness of God if it isn't a deep sense of wonder
at the world he has made?

---

[1] Michel Quoist, From *Prayers,* © Sheed and Ward, Inc., 1963.

Chapter 3

The Miracle of Persons

THE SENSE OF WONDER—and persons. Is there anything in all creation more wonderful than persons? The artists among us— the painters, sculptors, photographers, novelists, dramatists especially—reserve a special place for these, for they are the most complex, the most fascinating, the most difficult to render of all God's creatures.

"What is man," asked the psalmist, "that thou art mindful of him? Thou hast made him a little lower than the angels." *That* in a day and in a culture where angels represented man's shiningest dreams of perfection!

No matter how many people I meet, I never cease to be amazed at the variety, the intricacy, the sheer miracle of them. Actually there are very few people on the face of the earth who are not worth a lifetime of study. You meet them everywhere— in pubs, churches, prisons, hospitals, on buses, trains, airplanes —everywhere that people go. I remember once when we were riding second class on a train from Paris to London and sat in a compartment with a poor peasant fellow. He was a sturdily built man with simple, childlike eyes set deep within the folds of a face that was weather-worn and timeless. What eyes they were! Even when the face was impassive, they looked out at you like two small animals watching from their lairs. As we were to learn, they had beheld much. The man was a Pole and had been deported to Siberia at the end of the second world war. When he was released from his frozen exile, he wandered across Europe and finally settled in Marseilles, where he put his understanding of farming to use as a gardener. He had married a girl from Italy, and her family lived with them. Now he was on his way to Liverpool to look for work in Great Britain because of the spiralling cost of living in France. When he had located something, he would go back to Marseilles and bring his wife along with him to their new home. He was an illiterate man, barely able to print the long name he bore when we were filling out passport papers, but he could speak six languages and had known suffering and love in all of them. We marveled at his unadorned good nature and gave thanks that we had not elected to ride in the first class coach where we would have missed him. When we left him in Victoria Station, we had a lump in our throats for the humanity to which we belonged.

I think of an old woman I met once in a church hall where she was painting quick little signs for a church bazaar. We fell to talking and I discovered that she was a real artist who enjoyed making signs because she had once supported herself and her invalid husband for four years in Chicago by doing commercial lettering of various kinds. Later she painted our sons' and my wife's portraits, and we spent many pleasant hours talking of her work and looking at the beautiful watercolors she had made all over Europe and the Near East, where she had lived virtually as a hobo during the twenty years since her husband's death. She was a magnificent person, both knowledgeable and spritely, and she shared herself completely with everybody she met.

It is a temptation to go on and on, rehearsing memories of

this person and that who has impressed me in some special way. It is so inspiring just to recall them. I remember, in spite of the world conditions that find their way so inevitably into the headlines of the newspapers, that the world is rich in beauty and kindness and heroism, in the little unremembered and unmemorialized acts of countless thousands of persons who live their lives with grace and style and humility. Thomas Gray knew what he was talking about in "An Elegy Written in a Country Churchyard"—only a minority of the great moments in human existence are ever recorded and known to the world at large. There are persons who are miracles all around us.

This was part of the remarkable genius of Jesus and of the writers of the Gospels, that they represented so consistently his painstaking concern for individuals. There is very little like this in the Old Testament. The psalms, which were canonized in Jewish history rather late, and thus to some extent form a bridge between the Old and the New Testaments, reveal a greater individualism than was common prior to that time. But in the ministry of Jesus it became apparent that every man was important in an eternal sense. The Gospels are full of vignettes describing the encounter of Christ with persons who are memorable precisely because they are not types but actual people. Our culture could never again be quite the same after that. Whenever anything has threatened personhood, whether it be slavery or conformity or military conscription or technology, it has come under the judgment of what we learned from Christ and the Incarnation. Everybody, every individual, is important to God.

This is hard for some people to believe. They want to believe it because it is comforting to do so. But they find it so unreasonable. How can we suppose that a single God, whom the Bible describes in highly personalistic terms, can possibly behold everybody everywhere at the same moment? It is really incredible.

C. S. Lewis has given what I believe is the best answer to this problem in his book *Mere Christianity*. We are so prone to try to subject God to our own space-time limitations and to imagine that he sees each of us the way we see one another, *ad seriatum* and in a segment of time. But God is the creator of all who dwell in time; he is not himself bound to it. Suppose, says Lewis, we think of a novelist writing a novel. He is not bound to the time limits of his characters. He may in fact take as long as he likes to describe something that transpires in their lives in only a few moments. He may even get up and stroll away in the midst of the description and return to it hours or maybe days later. Time is not the same for him; he is above it, beyond it, out of its reach. It is all a mystery, of course, but God is somehow beyond our way of marking time and space. He is eternal. And he is able to contemplate us in ways in which we are not really able to consider each other.

Doesn't this impart a dignity to each human life that it would not otherwise have? And if we remember this, doesn't it make other persons important as more than statistics or masses or cannon fodder or faceless integers on the way to a "great society"?

We are prone today to the same way of thinking that afflicted the ancient Greeks, when men conceived of model persons and despaired of all the people who did not attain to the ideal. We tend to measure the people we know by heroes and matinee idols. We do it even unconsciously at times. We are censorious and fault-finding because most of the individuals we know do not fit into the molds of our preconceived notions of what ideal humanity is. Men tend to estimate feminine attractiveness according to the standard of the *Playboy* foldout; as comedian Mort Shal once said, the average American boy grows up today thinking that the all-American girl has a staple in her navel. And we lack a fine sensitivity for what is unique and inimitable and in that sense perhaps even sacred in every person we meet, no matter how far from the narrowly conceived ideal he or she happens to be.

This kind of thinking is warped because it leads to the idolization of the creature and ignores the glory of the Creator. When

[66]

it is God who is central to our thinking, and not the creation, every person in the world assumes an interest for us, because he is then a priceless reflection of the One we can behold *only* through what he has created. The person who is different, who does not conform to a standardized image, is treasured for precisely that reason; he has something, he reveals something, that others do not share.

"I am a human being. Do not bend, staple, mutilate, or spindle." Thus reads the comic slogan one occasionally sees printed on colored buttons. And yet it is much more than a comic slogan. It has a deeply serious import, for it is the heart-cry of many people in modern society—of workers in unions, of students in universities, of wives in commuter societies, of children in busy families, of soldiers on alien soil, of vast numbers of people who have their own private interpretations of the evils of population explosion and the impersonalism of modern existence.

I am a human being. There is depth in that announcement, maybe more depth than I myself realize. At the very least, it means that my existence is more than mechanical, more than a formula, more than a numerical equation. It means that I—and all the other I's in the world—should be treated with respect for my mystery, for the thing about me that cannot be reduced to mechanics and formulas and equations.

Ironically, it is not the machine that treats persons as machines. An acquaintance of mine who is a computer expert corrected my thinking about this once after I had made some remark about the way we tend to "computerize" humanity today. The computer, he said, is far less likely than we are to judge men by superficial appearances; it is greedy for information, and then it uses information logically and without prejudice to project still further constructions about the person or persons under consideration. We human beings are the ones who tend to categorize others according to initial impressions, often blinding

[67]

ourselves forever to the real qualities they possess. We fix our attention upon a single characteristic—usually something that pleases us or displeases us very much—and from then on the only evidence we are interested in is that which corroborates what we had suspected all along.

But we miss so much when we do not meet what is really there in other people; we miss the richest part of human existence. What can we do to help ourselves to take advantage of the ability to relate to others and to enjoy the human experience more fully?

Surely the first thing to do is to realize how prone we are to live only on the surface of our relationships and not to explore them in depth. It is not an easy thing to admit to oneself that he has been barging along through life without any real sensitivity to the infinite number of possibilities around him. Yet that is precisely what each of us must admit. We cannot know how many times we have missed some life-changing experience because we were preoccupied with some personal matter and failed to respond with even a portion of our human potential to the potential that was in someone else. We touch so many people we never really meet, brush them in passing, even work beside them or live in the same house with them for years, and never discover the flame we might have kindled with them. We treat them as "its," said Martin Buber, and not as "thous."

I can never forget the letter I once read that a friend had written to the English theologian Herbert Farmer. The friend, a clergyman, said he had returned to his home late in the afternoon after a day of exhausting labor and had just loosened his tie and gotten comfortable when there was someone at the door. It was a frail little woman in very thick-lensed spectacles, being conducted by a thin, pasty-faced lad who was obviously her son. They were selling cotton goods from door to door. The clergyman was very tired, and he said he was afraid he cut short a tale of domestic woe with a very curt reply. The boy said to his mother, "Come away, mum," and led her back to the street. As they went through the front gate, the boy turned and looked back. There was an appearance of terrible hatred on his face. Too late the minister realized what he had done. In one thoughtless moment, when he believed himself too weary for another encounter with a human being whom he did not know, he had managed to enforce perhaps for a lifetime that boy's conviction that no man cares for another and that life is "red in tooth and claw." And then they were gone. He probably would never see them again. When the remorse of his failure had fully struck home to him, he turned into the house again and cried, "God have mercy on us all."

If we do not live with a kind of availability, ready to meet others when they are ready to be met, then we do not know how many times this very situation is our own. Sometimes we haven't even the power to recognize an opportunity that has just passed us by. Sometimes the needs are not so obvious as they were in this case. Sometimes our failure is not made plain in the pouting face of a child, because we are dealing with someone who has learned to dissemble, just as that boy would one day learn to seem impassive when disappointed in others. But life is a constant gamut of such experiences, and a man may make what he will of it. The more we learn to watch and to listen, to use our eyes and ears to get outside of ourselves, the more we will discover the inestimable richness of being human.

It is a good practice, I think, not disregarding another person's more obvious qualities, always to look for his hidden ones. It is like a wonderful game, maybe of the kind they play in heaven. I had a friend once who became marvelously adept at it. He seemed to have an instinct for ferreting out bits of information and clues to secret traits in the people he met. Then he flattered these people about these relatively unpublic things. It had an almost incredible effect on people; they were pleased beyond words at the interest he showed in them. I realized, after being around him for a while, that it isn't the big things in people's lives that they like to be praised for, the well known facts, the obvious abilities, the much publicized accomplishments, but the little things that usually escape notice, things that in people's own eyes are really the keys to their inner selves.

I know a young man who is a musician of unusual talent. He has already had great experience as a conductor of choruses and orchestras. Yet it pleases him far more to be complimented as a chef than as a conductor, for at home he dotes on baking bread and preparing exotic foodstuffs. Another man is an engineer who has lived all over the world and now has a very responsible position with an international organization; yet nothing pleases him more than for someone to appreciate the sensitiveness of the poetry he scribbles in the late hours of the night. Still another man is a sales manager for a well known company in a very large territory; he has an excellent reputation as an aggressive businessman, but the pride of his life is his green thumb— he grows the most gorgeous roses I have ever seen.

It is this way with most of the people we know. There are things about them one never sees in meeting them casually. You have to follow a man home into the interior of his being to really become acquainted with him. And it's a little hard to speak of loving people if you don't do this.

Our tragedy is compounded, of course, by the fact that we are often insensitive to those who are closest of all to us. Psychiatrists and ministers are well accustomed to hearing from persons they are counseling the testimony that their husbands or wives do not really know them at all. We are so likely to take for granted the thoughts and beliefs and desires of those with whom we consider our acquaintance to be most intimate, never bothering to say, "What do you really think about this question," or, if we do ask, never bothering to listen to the answer. As a result, marriages grow stale and relationships between parents and children become calloused and insensitive, and we are bored with our families because all we really see in them are our own ricocheted ideas and feelings. We are like so many quicksilver globules racing around in a house-sized container, always bumping into one another but never really fusing.

Not long ago there was an editorial in a popular magazine about the new look in family relations today. It alluded to many things, including the problems of commuter fathers and suburban mothers; but mainly it stressed the arrival of real democracy in the modern home, with fathers and mothers sharing the decision-making and other responsibilities with the children. The following week the "Letters to the Editor" column carried a rather long and touching letter from a college girl who wanted to commend the "new attitude" in parent-child relations. She said that she had grown up in a well-to-do home with rather strict parents who had always told her what to do and what to think. Whenever she tried to express herself on a subject, her father would say something like, "What do you know about it?" or "You're stupid; when we want your opinion we'll ask for it." Although the girl's letter was couched in terms of resentment, it was plain that she longed for a wholesome relationship with her parents. She needed to be able to share with them, to give herself to them and to have them in return.

I was moved by the girl's letter, not just because I felt sorry for her, but because I realized that I as a parent am often tempted to take the same line with my children. I don't mean to. There is really nothing in the world that is good for them that I wouldn't try to do for them. But sometimes, in my own weariness or lethargy, I fail to be as open to them as I should. When they come banging up to me with all the noise and energy of their young years, I retreat behind a wall of stuffiness and dismiss questions with off-handed answers or turn away enthusiasm with a grunt. It is an ugly picture of myself, and I would prefer not to see it. But I had better see it! I had better see it and realize that it is the picture of a murderer, who slowly but methodically kills what is youthful and ebullient and exciting in people. How much better am I, really, than the man who takes a gun or a knife and brings the stumbling life of a corpse to an end? For I have killed what is dearer—the soul and spirit of the young in heart.

The point is that in all human relationships a man must pay a price in strength and energy or fail to carry off his end of the bargain. Sharing is costly. It means vigilance, that we may see the needs and desires of others. It means empathy, that we may genuinely feel their situations. And it means sacrifice, that we may actually join them in those situations and share our own resources with them.

Sometimes we won't even take the first step. We don't want to see the suffering of others because it is unpleasant and we don't want to become involved in it. We are afraid to become entangled. We are like the priest and the Levite in the story of the Good Samaritan, who walked on the other side of the way rather than become engaged in the plight of a man lying broken and in need beside the road.

The problem is that we die a little bit every time we take the other side of the way. We are so constituted as human beings that we realize our humanness only when we share it with other persons. We have a habit of explaining our faults by saying, "Oh, that is just human." But the truth is that being human is really a positive thing, not a negative one, and we discover it whenever we do something courageous or worthwhile in the human community—responding to the need of a child or the loneliness of a fellow creature.

A university professor in a southwestern community shared this with me. He said that there were two ways he could travel from his office to his home in the afternoon. One was down wide, tree-lined boulevards where the homes were lovely and spacious and the children played in sandboxes and rode bikes on the sidewalks. The other was through the narrow, crooked lanes of the city ghetto, where children milled around garbage cans and chased each other around an occasional cinder-packed lot. If

he took the first, there was nothing to interrupt his late afternoon euphoria all the way from the university parking lot to the
driveway of his own pleasant home in the suburbs. If he took the
second, he said, he couldn't get the scenes out of his mind even
long after he had gone to bed at night; they haunted his con-
science until he couldn't rest.

Now which way elicited the man's humanity more? Through
the pleasant middle-class district, or through the ghetto? The
answer you give may betray how much you have learned about
life—and about being human.

What does the church have to do with being human? Is it
really concerned with such a question? Maybe it is more interested in making us divine, or something like that.

Before we answer the question, we ought perhaps to ask what
Jesus' own attitude toward it seems to have been. What was he
after, anyway? Was he really interested in an institution that
would proscribe rather narrowly the boundaries of human nature, and give glory to God, so to speak, by pinching man? Did
he conceive of the church as a kind of ethical and creedal mold
for turning out men and women who all acted and thought just
alike?

Think, now. That is what we have so often taken the church
to be. We have identified it not with freedom but with the loss
of freedom. We have thought of it as an organization more or
less resistant to change and insensitive to human individuality.
Many of us carry around considerable burdens of guilt-feeling
because our real faces underneath do not conform to the masks
we wear when we are with other church folk. We are not quite
sure how to go about it, but we expect that when we belong to
the church we are supposed to be more than merely human, or
at least other than merely human. We quote St. Paul to the
effect that we are not to be conformed to this world, but to be
transformed by the renewing of our minds and spirits—only, by

the time we are through, we have usually managed to make of the transforming only another kind of conformity, invested with all sorts of rigamaroles and requirements.

But what about Jesus? Isn't the first thing that must be said about him the fact that he never regarded religion as an end in itself, but only as a means to an end? He was always contradicting the religious people of his day. They had got it all backwards, he said; they had got the idea that man is made for the sake of religion, when the truth is that religion is only something to help man be a true man. It was no little part of providence that Jesus came from Nazareth, a rough northern town where social etiquette and the finer points of the religious law were not regarded for themselves. This was one reason that many of the priests and scribes at Jerusalem reacted to him so strongly; in their eyes, he belonged to an irrepressibly rowdy and unsophisticated tradition, one not at all in agreement with the more genteel ways of the Holy City. But the Holy City needed his irreverence—needed it like a good shot of reality. All religions tend to become bogged down in rules and customs, and to lose sight of the unpretentious, human side of their beginnings. Jesus was a true man, and the first thing he demanded of his own religion was humanity. Anything else was a falsehood, even if it was perpetrated in the name of God. True religion to him did not mean the restoration of Paradise—that had become the false assumption of the Jews—it meant the restoration of Adam! *Man* must come back. He must become what God had created him to be. That was the thing of prime importance.

And that is why Jesus seemed to be so much more interested in behavior than he was in the Law. How people acted was the thing that absorbed his attention. The parables, which constitute some of the greatest teaching the world has ever known, more often than not were stories about people so real and human you could almost reach out and touch them. Relationship was so much more important than theology in his thinking. There was nothing academic or artificial in his approach to problems. It was real. It was gripping. Or, in an appropriate metaphor, it was "down to earth."

Take the story of the Good Samaritan, for example, which we mentioned a few pages back. A lawyer who was concerned to ascertain for himself the wisdom and shrewdness of this widely publicized teacher from the northern territories had put the question to Jesus about which is the greatest commandment. It was not really a new question. It was the sort of thing the rabbis debated rather commonly in those days. And Jesus' answer, that the greatest commandment is to love God and that the other side of the same commandment is to love the neighbor, was probably not an especially original one. What was original, what went beyond mere theology and got an unshakeable grip on the imagination of the lawyer that day, was the story which Jesus told to illustrate the meaning of neighborhood. That, after all, was where the commandments always bogged down, when men began to rationalize away their applicability.

In about one minute, Jesus had put the whole commandment, even the part about loving God, into an unforgettable perspective. A certain man, traveling from Jericho to Jerusalem, had been set upon by brigands who took everything he had and left him nearly dead. A priest came along the road, where he could not help seeing the man, but he kept right on going. Ditto a Levite. There was the religious establishment in a nutshell. It had other fish to fry. Then a Samaritan happened along. Enter drama. The Jews contemned Samaritans. They were a bastard race. Their customs were peculiar. They were not to be trusted. But bang!—the Samaritan stopped to help the unfortunate traveler. He took him to a hostel and paid his board and room while he was recuperating, promising even that if more was required he would pay it on the way back.

There it was, inescapably. The demands of God are in terms of concrete, specific relationships with other men. No amount of talking about God and the Bible and ethics and theology is equal to the smallest action taken in behalf of another human being.

[75]

And we have never been able to get this burr from under our saddle!

I remember D. T. Niles telling the story once of a man who had been converted in a Billy Graham meeting in a city in India. The man was hurrying along the dark streets afterwards when he almost fell over a beggar sitting beside the way asking alms. He paused just long enough to say to the man, "I'm sorry, my friend, I would like to stop and help you, but I have just found Christ this evening, and I am in a great hurry to reach home and tell my wife and children about it." Niles' wry comment was, "He had just missed Christ where he might have found him—in the beggar along his way."

No, the church does not exist merely to confess something, to say that it believes something; it exists to *do* something. It exists to be Christ to the world. It exists to renew man's relationship to man and man's relationship to God by *acting out* these relationships. Dietrich Bonhoeffer called it our *deputyship*—we are God's deputies, acting for him in the world to make men whole again, to provide companionship, to bring back love.

I have always wondered if the church didn't forget one of the sacraments. We observe the sacraments of baptism and communion because we say they were instituted by Christ and he commanded us to continue them. But according to a tradition recorded in the Fourth Gospel, there was something he did just before eating that last meal with the disciples that could just as easily have become a sacrament. He took a towel and a basin of water and washed the disciples' feet. And afterwards, as they sat at the table, he said, "You ought to do as I have done to you." There is a small sect known as "foot-washing Baptists" that still observes this practice today; the members begin their meetings by washing each other's feet. But even though the practice never became widespread, the spirit of it ought to be preserved in every gathering of the church. We are servants to the world, not lords. We bring love to the world by *being* love to the world.

There is a picture of what we are supposed to be and do for

the world in something a group of college students did one Christmas in a church in Paris. They had just had a Christmas Eve dinner and there was a lot of food left over. One of the students, a little Jewish girl, asked the pastor of the church if they couldn't go out and find some *clochards,* or beggars, to come in and eat it. He agreed, and the students went out. By and by they began to return with their *clochards.* Some they had found sleeping under the bridges of the Seine. One had been curled up in a toolbox along the quay. He had been reluctant to come, lest someone else take his place for the night. Several men were brought from the jail, where they had been taken in for the night. It was an amazing sight to behold—men whose clothes were in tatters, burlap wrapped around their feet like great bandages, their hair tangled and uncut, their faces encrusted in dirt and whiskers, looking about them incredulously, unable to believe that anyone could be doing them a favor without working an angle of some sort. They went into a rest room and washed their hands and faces. One of them passed around a comb he had in his pocket. And soon they sat down to the first Christmas meal most of them had had in years. One man ate three bowls of soup—he did not know that there would be other courses to follow. Halfway through his main course, he was unable to eat another bite. He excused himself from the table, went into the rest room, put his finger down his mouth, regurgitated, and returned to finish what was on his plate. One old man, who had been a professional violinist before falling on evil days, cried all the way through the meal. The students had never seen anything like it. Most of them were themselves quite poor, but they had never dreamed that men like these existed. They all said it was the finest Christmas they had ever had.

It is an extreme picture, admittedly; the church's ministry to the world calls for much more than a soup line on the eve of a holy day. But it is an important picture to get once in a while. Important because there is a sense in which every man who comes into the church is a *clochard,* a man destitute and begging for assistance. We are an organization of beggars, and we share what we have willingly with all the others. Some really do need food. Others need companionship. Others need guidance. Others need a chance to give themselves.

What was Robert Frost's great line about home, that it's where, when you go there, they have to take you in? Well, church is where, when you go there, they *want* to take you in. They want to because they've all been taken in themselves, at one time or another.

Are we ready to talk about *love?* It is a difficult subject, and one we probably ought never to approach except as we see it incarnate. Otherwise, we become sentimental about it, speak rhetorically, and miss it by a hundred miles. But if we saw an illustration of it in the story of the *clochards,* perhaps we can speak of it here.

It is a funny thing that we should speak of "falling in love," as though coming to love were an easy or even an unavoidable thing to do. Actually, this is far from true. What this metaphor really describes is enchantment, not love. Love is not something you fall into. As Rainer Maria Rilke said in a letter to a young friend, "For one human being to love another . . . is perhaps the most difficult of all our tasks, the ultimate, the last test and proof, the work for which all other work is but preparation." That is a proper assessment—we work all our lives preparing to love.

Maybe this is why the First Epistle of John says that we know God only if we love—and then says that God *is* love. These sayings are deceptively simple. There is never a time when we do not think we know what they mean. But I am becoming convinced that they are really expressions of mystical truths—insights attained only by the man who loves. That man, having felt the raw, unorganized impressions of what love is, hears the gospel of the Incarnation, and then he knows the name of what it is he has been feeling—it is God.

Take this experience of a young man I know as an example.

[78]

He had spent the summer drifting through the lands around the eastern end of the Mediterranean Sea and found himself in a certain city penniless and very lonely. He had had only a sandwich to eat during the past five days. In a depressed and listless state of mind, he strolled along the beach, thinking how hard the world is. Suddenly a minor commotion occurred in front of him. A man who had been swimming in the sea came out to find that someone had stolen all of his clothing and his money; all he had left was the rather skimpy swimsuit he was wearing. But then a quiet miracle occurred. Someone took off a part of his own clothing and gave it to the man. Another person did the same, and another and another. Soon the poor man was completely outfitted and was able to depart for home. It all happened in a moment. Instinctively the boy thought: "It is of God." He had *named* the wonderful act he had seen. And he went on his way with a new spirit.

What is real love? How can we define it? A friend of mine who is a wonderful marriage and family counselor states it as basically as he can: Love is a yearning of the separated for reunion. My friend was a chaplain on a navy carrier during the second world war and observed the reactions of men away from home and families. What was it, he kept asking himself, that made these sailors think so constantly of what was back there on the other side of the ocean? The only answer was that they felt that they belonged together with what was back there. They belonged with friends and family but had been wrenched away by the fact of a war. And now their hearts returned instinctively to the persons they had left behind.

Love is the desire to get back together again. The observation my friend made in the war has exceptional possibilities as a definition, it seems to me, for it applies to a wide range of situations, from marriage and family relationships to spiritual and theological understandings. It is mirrored in any person's feelings for his family. It is reflected in the Peace Corps volunteer's sense of mission in another part of his world. It is idealized

[79]

—and mythologized—in the coming of God in Christ and the death of Christ on the Cross for the atonement (at-one-ment) of the world. Love is the discovery of all the interrelatedness of the world. It is what the boy saw on the beach as a vision—the understanding that we are all together and are to share what we have with each other.

What this says is that there is a basic oneness to creation, a wholeness that we often fail to realize because of our own fragmentedness and isolation. It is when we begin to love, to yearn for union with someone or something beyond ourselves, that we begin to see this. Then we no longer feel alone. Even the man who is in love with a woman has a sense of well-being in the world, as if there were a harmony of design and purpose about it even though invisible. He moves with a sense of comfort and warmth in his surroundings, confident that life means well. Perhaps this is why in the Carson McCullers-Edward Albee play *Ballad of a Sad Cafe* there is an enigmatic speech about love in which it is said that most people would rather love than be loved. I questioned that at first, but now I see that it is right. To be in love is to feel the underlying unity of existence, whether the love is returned or not. It is to be aware of relationship. To be loved, in comparison, is nothing.

When I was a young seminarian, I read Anders Nygren's great book *Agape and Eros,* in which a rigid distinction is drawn between worldly, acquisitive love (*eros*) and the free, unselfish love of which the New Testament usually speaks (*agape*). Nygren made it especially plain that the love of God is of a spontaneous nature and is never generated by anything outside of God. When a man realizes what God has done for him in Christ, he then becomes a channel of this ungenerated love and is able to love the world.

I was bothered for years by what I read in that book. I realized that my love was erotic to a degree, but I did not think it was all that acquisitive; and, for the life of me, I didn't honestly know how to go about being a better channel for a love that was

[80]

spontaneous and couldn't be prompted anyway. I felt that I was sort of stuck. I couldn't go backwards and I couldn't go forwards. If Nygren was right, most of my attempts at loving were selfish and only God could do anything about the kind of love that isn't!

But now that I have gotten over a little of my country-boy's reverence for the printed page and for the word of noted theologians, I am able to see the very first mistake that Nygren made—in dividing love into spiritual and earthly kinds to begin with. It was a mistake because love can never really be divided into categories like that. That is a devil's trick theologians have been playing for centuries in order to keep some kind of demarcation going between the sacred order and the secular order. The truth is that love is all of a piece—sexual love, familial love, brotherly love, tribal love, God-love, self-love—it is all a yearning for reunion expressed at different levels and in different manners. And this is an extremely important thing to remember, for it permits us to accept even less commendable varieties of love as basically positive signs and not negative ones. A man who loves his wife dearly but seems to hate the rest of the world, for example, need not think of his love for his wife as an indication of his selfishness; he may regard it instead as one area of relationship where he is more successful than in other areas, and it may thereby become the thing he needs to make a transition to the other areas as well. Any kind of love, when it is recognized as the search for relationship, may well become the analogy by which an individual is able to move on to other and more inclusive forms of love. For what happens, in effect, is that the person begins to see himself as one who loves, that is, as one who yearns for larger relationships; and the very fact of his having that image of himself enables him to approach the problem of relationship with new spirit and new understanding.

I think the thing that especially crystallized my objection to Nygren's bifurcated approach to love was a little passage in Frankl's reflections on prison life, which I have mentioned before. In this passage Frankl was describing an all night forced march which he and other prisoners made one winter, tramping along, up hill and down, through ice and frost and cold water. What kept the poor undernourished creatures going? Strangely, a fellow prisoner near to Frankl, stumbling along on that bitterly cold and exhausting exodus, spoke of his wife, and Frankl realized that the same dream was preserving them both. Frankl didn't know where his own wife was, or whether she was even alive; he had not seen her for over three years. But that did not matter. He clung to the image he had of her anyway. She was a unit of relationship in a world where so few could be trusted, where relationship was likely to spell sudden death. And Frankl said, "The salvation of man is through love and in love." That was the truth he had learned in all his bitter experience in the death camps.

Like that line in *The Ballad of a Sad Cafe,* this observation shocked me a bit at first. It spoke of the world's being saved by love, and my mind immediately thought of an ethereal, heavenly kind of love, or at least of an altruistic, sacrificial kind of love. But no! that wasn't what he meant at all. He had just been speaking of his vision of his wife. It was a very common kind of love, perhaps even a selfish kind. There was nothing other-worldly about it, nothing "spiritual," nothing religious.

But then I began to realize that the trouble with half of our concepts of love is their idealism. We form them so remote from reality, so far from where we actually live. And here was a beginning, a very concrete and specific place to start. If we really mean to love, to improve our relationship to the world we live in, then we must not ignore the necessity of such a beginning. A man who is not very serious about the quality of his relationship with his wife, or his children, or his working associates, is only deluding himself if he dreams of relationships on a grander scale.

Chapter 4

The Human Depths of the Scriptures

A FEW PAGES BACK I referred to the Bible. I realize that that is a dangerous thing for a writer. It could easily have turned off many readers. As the teen-agers say, we don't "dig" the Bible much anymore. It seems so archaic in an age of synthetic fibers, wonder drugs, and instant communication, like some Oriental gong sounding out of a distant and shadowy past. What could it possibly say to modern man?

I was sitting at dinner with a bank official recently, and he made the remark that he reads a page or two of Montaigne every night before going to bed. Someone else asked if he reads the Bible. He replied that he does not read it very often anymore, even though he is a very religious man. "The Old Testament is completely closed to me now," he said. "I find nothing there but a lot of tribalism. And as for the New Testament, I can endure very little of it except the Gospels and the Acts of the Apostles, and I have just about had it with the Acts of the Apostles."

Another friend who travels a great deal in airplanes says that whenever he is very tired and wishes to relax and not talk to fellow passengers, he takes out a Bible and spreads it open in his lap. It works like a charm, he says. Nobody ever speaks to him.

"The Holy Bible," we stamp on the cover of it. "Holy"—sacred, transcendent, supernatural, divine. And there is absolutely no use in reading it in an age when our holiest task is to become more human.

Or is there?

Is the Bible really about God? Not long ago I heard it described from a pulpit as "the record of man's search for God." A century ago, maybe even a generation ago, that is what we were saying about it. But to be quite honest today, it is only partially about God, isn't it? It is mostly about man—about man stumbling, running, satisfied, frustrated, drunken, sober, open, pretentious, alert, inert, scheming, innocent, clean, dirty, caring, mean, daring, denying, living, dying: about man praising and blaspheming, believing and doubting, blessing and cursing. It is about man, pious and impious; about MAN in capital letters, man as Miguel de Unamuno celebrated him, a creature of flesh and blood, man here and now, real and specific, living, breathing, agonizing, rejoicing, man of the earth!

And that is why it is important that we not discard this book in an age of humanism, that we not allow it to languish as a dust-gatherer and fetish, as the least-read best selling book in the world. And it is also why it is important that the clergy stop reading it and talking about it as if it were some thunder-charged tome set over against man for keeping him in order and condemning him when he is out of order, or as if it were some cabalistic scroll reserved for the understanding and interpretation of priests and theologians alone. I could hardly believe my ears when a Protestant minister actually complained to me once that his people wanted to meet together in groups to discuss the Bible. "It is too specialized," he said. "They cannot possibly understand what it is all about." What is special in the Bible

is its view of man, a view that has informed the greatest literature of the Western world for nearly two millenia, including the
writings of Dante, Chaucer, Shakespeare, Milton, Melville, Tol-
stoy and Dostovsky. It is a view of man as the glorious and
inglorious creature of God, sometimes worthy, sometimes unworthy, but always interesting and exciting because of that. Maybe
laymen will puzzle at some of the language and syntax of the
Scriptures, and perhaps even at some of the mystifying cultural
mores—but these are things that puzzle scholars too. What it
would do for a layman's confidence to attend a professional
meeting of ministers or theologians sometime and hear the
disputations, often endless, on nearly every subject under consideration! The important thing about the Bible is that from beginning to end, from garden to garden, it is the story of man Oh,
there are some prior things to be got out of the way in Genesis
—animals, rivers, seas, and so on, all the facts surrounding man
—but they are dispatched in double-quick order. And once
man's tale is started, we never get away from it!

Some people get upset at finding anything in the Scriptures
they can't agree with, as if it had to be all of a piece, double or
nothing. I wonder if they feel the same way about their daily
newspaper or their school books. That would make it awfully
difficult to proceed in life.

A lot of persons, since the teachings of evolution began to take
effect, have hit a major obstacle right in the beginning of the
Bible—the story of Adam and Eve. The carbon-dating process
has enabled us to determine rather precisely when certain skeletons and artifacts discovered here and there were actually part of
the scene, and some of these evidently go back many hundreds
of thousands of years—certainly well beyond the 6,000 years or
so over which the famous Bishop Ussher strung out the biblical
records. And enough skeletons and pieces of skeletons have been
found to verify beyond any scientific doubt the hypotheses con-
cerning the development of man from a pre-literate and probably

even pre-lingual species. Adam and Eve, to an era as sophisticated in laboratory techniques as ours, do begin to sound like a gross over-simplification.

But are they any less true? Bishop John A. T. Robinson, speaking to this point in his book *But That I Can't Believe!* asks if the popular British couple Andy and Flo Capp are any less true because they are in the comic strips and do not exist as real people with a street address and a telephone number. Americans might ask the same about Dagwood and Blondie Bumstead. We have chortled over Dagwood's quandaries and defeats for years —precisely because his situations always ring so true! In a sense, he is more true for being unreal; he is able to embody the problems and *faux pas* of millions of folk at a time!

For some persons, Adam and Eve are only products of the fertile primitive imagination, and are therefore not to be taken seriously. These persons prefer their truth to be direct and factual, without any playing around. But some truth is just too big and too important to be got at so directly. On a smaller scale, we surround ourselves with "imaginary" creatures from childhood to the grave—the Tooth Fairy, the Bogey Man, Santa Claus, Justice, Liberty, the State, and so on. The list is practically endless. Most of these fabricated beings have some touch of reality about them. They have to, else we wouldn't have them. They enable us to deal with reality, to talk about it, to contend with it, to use it in being persons. But as to being something that can be weighed on the scales or photographed with a camera or shut up in a box—well, that is something else again. Their reality in a sense depends on their ability to *transcend* reality, to get beyond the individual and specific instances.

"Adam" is the Hebrew word for man; and, before that, it was probably the word for a kind of ruddy-colored clay. The creature whom God was depicted as fashioning from the dust of the ground was called Adam—*man*. And the wife whom God formed of the rib taken from his side was called Eve, which in Hebrew meant *life*. She was to be mate and mother, and life was to go on through her. A man knows what that means every time he sits in a hospital lobby and waits for word from the maternity ward. It is a miracle.

Now is the story of Adam and Eve any less true for that? I should hope to say not!

Here is what I picture: Some little Jewish chap (I say Jewish because this particular account of the creation eventually came to us through the Jews) one day asked his mother one of those incredibly difficult questions that children always have a way of asking until they grow up a bit and learn that their parents really don't know and can't answer them. He said, "Mama, where did I come from?" That wasn't too hard, and she answered it. Then he said, "Mama, where did you and papa come from?" That wasn't hard either, and she answered it. But by the time the child had carried the exercise back through a dozen generations, mama got tired of answering and said what mamas everywhere say when they get tired. She said, "I don't know, dear, why don't you run along and ask your papa?" Which he did. Doubtless he expected papa to keep going back too, for it was a nice game. But papa, as papas do, had a more direct way of answering the question than mama, for he could see where the game could lead and did not think he had time for such games. So papa headed for the pass, as we say. He went directly back to the source of all the children and children's children in the world. And to talk about the first man and the first woman, he needed more than ordinary names. He couldn't just call the first man Reuben, and he couldn't just call the first woman Leah. He had to be more definitive than that. He probably would have called the man Abram, "father of the people," but even the child knew that Abram (or Abraham) was a historical person, and if the papa had called the man that the child would have naturally said, "And where did Abram come from?" The simplest solution was to call the first man Adam, for it not only gave him the generic name but indicated his origin as well. Or it did almost. Just in time, papa realized he would have to explain where dust came from, so he went back one step further and talked about how the world came into being.

"But what about God? Where did he come from?" Can't you hear the child asking that? Ah, but here the father was on firm footing at last. "God, my son? God didn't come from anywhere. He always was. He is God."

Well, maybe it was something like that. And maybe papa made the mistake of putting Adam and Eve in the Garden of Eden because he always dreamed of youth and beauty and innocence and leisure, and then had to respond to the child's questioning about why they didn't all live in paradise now, all his uncles and aunts and grandparents and cousins, who were all descendants of Adam and Eve. What did take away Paradise, anyway? The disobedience of the first man and woman? Their desire to overleap themselves and be like God? Isn't this what always takes away a man's paradise? Isn't the story repeated in every one of us, age after age?

We don't read the Bible, said Kierkegaard: *it reads us*. And it does, doesn't it? Reads us like open books.

Maybe this is important. Maybe it helps us to know who we are as persons, and *how* we are.

I once heard a minister denounce a C. B. DeMille biblical epic he had seen at a local movie house. What do you suppose had upset him about the picture? The crude modernization of primitive and ritual belief? The facile, Hollywoodish good looks of the leading actors and actresses? The mellow baritone voice of God dubbed in from offscreen from time to time? No, it wasn't any of these things. What really bothered the cleric was a wild, orgiastic dance scene in which some wriggling, twisting belly dancers slithered and gyrated to the accompaniment of a crescendo of drum beats. "There is no place in a biblical film," he declared uncompromisingly, "for such a blatant display of sexuality."

Well, now. I wondered if this fellow had ever read the Bible.

Really read it, not just opened it to certain sections and repeated parrot-like the particular texts which bolstered his own ethical and theological opinions. Read it like Kierkegaard said, so that it read him. Because somehow he had missed many of the richest parts of the Old Testament.

Like the story of how Abraham told everybody down in Egypt that Sarah was really his sister, and not his wife, because he knew they would kill him for her great beauty (Genesis 12). Or Joseph and Potipher's wife (Genesis 39). Or Rahab the harlot (Joshua 1). Or Samson and Delilah (Judges 16). Or the rape of the poor concubine of Gibeah (Judges 19). Or the seizing of the girls of Shiloh as they danced in the annual festival of Yahweh (Judges 21). Or David and the wife of Uriah (2 Samuel 11). Or Solomon and his foreign women (1 Kings 11).

There is little in James Bond that is more colorful than some of this material from the pages of the Old Testament!

Maybe the minister I mentioned had the problem so many people have had, of regarding the Bible as a book actually written by God and not by man, so that he could not even imagine its containing anything below his own moral standards. I met a woman once who was wrestling with this problem. She was living through a period of great personal difficulty and had begun to read the Bible again after a lapse of several years, thinking that would help her. She had read as far as the twelfth chapter of Genesis, where she encountered that story of Abraham's deceit about Sarah's relationship to him in order to avoid death at the hands of the Egyptians. Abraham had actually let his wife go to the pharaoh's court as one of the royal women. "I don't understand," said the puzzled woman. "That wasn't right! How could God ever use a man who would do a thing like that?" She had never expected to find anything immoral or unseemly between the covers of the Bible.

This is a common problem among people who think of the Bible as a stultifying book of rules and prohibitions. They have always been hung up on the Ten Commandments or the regulations of temple worship or the moralistic insertions of some of the redactors of the historical material, and have missed the intensely colorful and human qualities of the Scriptures. If they had read the Bible more sensitively, as they would have read a novel or a history book, they would have realized that the Ten Commandments, for example, do not stand alone as a great implacable law code suddenly delivered out of the blue for all mankind, becoming thus the inflexible standard and inevitable judge to condemn every man who doesn't fulfill them. They would have seen, on the contrary, that the commandments came as a necessity to an almost hopelessly disorganized and undisciplined people trying to make a go of it in a wild, nomadic situation. In this sense, the commandments were an act of grace on God's part, not of sullen legalism! They helped the Israelites to *survive*. Without them, there probably would never have been a nation of Israel.

There are so many misconceptions of what the Bible is and how it ought to be regarded today. Some people have made it into a sort of talisman, a protector of the home and the family (why else do we continue to record wedding dates and birth dates in the flyleaves of expensive, seldom read Bibles?), and a lucky rabbit's foot for soldiers in battle zones. There are even persons who consult the Bible as a decision-maker, the way the fabulous Doctor Dolittle discovered which way to take his next voyage out of the mapbook, by sticking a pin in a page without looking and then assuming that the spot where the pin landed was a supernaturally intended message.

If only these persons knew a little more of how the Bible came to us—of the process of canonization, the absence of original manuscripts, the unreliability of the men who copied the manuscripts (sometimes they were illiterate!), the problems of selecting the best of variable editions, the problems of interpreting meaning and providing accurate translations. Problems, problems, problems. The way is beset by problems! It is so hard to believe, in the face of this, that there are still millions of people who would insist to the death that every word in a certain version of the Scriptures is just exactly "what God intended it to be," as though he personally had written it. That is a kind of biblical illiteracy that is just as bad as the kind in which people have not even read the Scriptures.

How much more meaning the pages of the Bible begin to assume when we read them as the writings of real men, men of flesh and blood, men with hopes and anxieties, strengths and weaknesses, beliefs and doubts akin to our own. Then we begin to understand the dynamic nature of faith that somehow binds us together with the saints in all the ages. We are not a people cut off from the stream of holiness and revelation. We stand in a place where we can look down and see that stream winding this way and that, past Abraham and Moses and David and Paul and Augustine and Bernard and Luther and Calvin and Wesley and Brooks and Temple, right down to where it flows by our own feet. God is not some once vocal deity who was always intervening in life and thought during a particular period of history but has since become remote and silent. He has not changed. It is the witness to him that has been uneven, that has produced sudden spurts and then inexplicable hiatuses. God does not depend on the Scriptures for his validation; they depend upon him!

It is a fact of life that the orthodoxy of one age becomes the heresy of the next, and the heresy of one age the orthodoxy of another. For, consider, when anything becomes orthodox it has the power of authority to bind men's thinking, and when men's thinking is arrested, when it is hung up on something, when men begin to insist that all men agree on a particular way of looking at the world, that is archest heresy. And when heretical ideas, on the other hand, become popular and widespread, they tend to become the common way of looking at the world, and hence orthodox. Thus is provided for the pattern of the establishment and disestablishment in every generation.

See what happens, then, when we invest the Scriptures with

the sense of orthodoxy. We have suddenly calcified their meaning, so that they cannot breathe with all the vigor and humanness of their original composition. We have frozen them in mid-flight, much as one might "freeze" out of a moving film a single frame of a bird on the wing.

This is a perfectly natural phenomenon, of course, and it occurs in any kind of literary criticism. A school of critics, or perhaps even one well-known critic, will make a pronouncement about the meaning of a particular poem or play. For years, this is the accepted interpretation of the writing. No one bothers to question it. The meaning of the piece is arrested. Everyone assumes he knows what it is. Then one day a brazen new critic challenges the old assumptions. "The author did not mean this at all," he says. "What he really intended was. . . ." And suddenly the whole piece comes alive again and speaks with new force, a force that was probably latent in it all along, waiting to be touched into life by a new insight, a new way of seeing, a new manner of interpretation.

We must understand that it is the same with the Bible. We read it differently in every age and nation according to who we are, to what we bring to the reading. And that is no derogation of the Scriptures! On the contrary, to insist on their unilateralness, their unquestionable orthodoxy, is to rob them of their real interest and excitement. The Bible is not a stale and stagnant book of religion. It throbs with the heartbeat of man. In many ways, it is as secular and profane a book as was ever written. And it deserves the chance to be what it is.

Consider the Psalms, for example. Many people don't really know the Psalms. They know the famous Shepherd Psalm (23) and perhaps the Pentitent Psalm (51) and snatches of other Psalms like the eighth and the 24th and 100th. But they never realize how remarkably varied the Psalms are, how questioning some of them are, or how bitter, or how pugnacious, or how totally egocentric. Read them through sometime at a sitting— they are considerably briefer than a novel or the Sunday edition of the *New York Times*. You will be amazed at the utter humanity of them. Some of them celebrate wealth and friends; some complain of ill health; some even rail against God as an absentee God! No one who is conversant with the Psalms will be shocked by the news of the death of God; the theme is not new at all. Imagine *arguing with God!* Yet some of those old Hebrew poets did. It is a wonderful insight into the nature of their religion. They might stand in awe of God from time to time, but it did not diminish their strong individuality.

I think this is why Bonhoeffer said in his *Letters and Papers from Prison* that most of us try to get to the New Testament too fast today, and must go back and come by way of the Old Testament. We are always reading the new back into the old, and spiritualizing the events and sayings of the old. But those events and sayings must stand as they were, unabashedly secular and worldly. Reading them for what they were, we will be saved from our modern docetism that would separate religion from where people really live.

A few years ago I read a manuscript for a publishing house which was considering publishing it. It was a book about the Bible in modern literature. Chapter by chapter, it dealt with contemporary novels and plays that have been based primarily on biblical episodes. I don't remember too many of them now. I am sure Thomas Mann's Joseph novels were there, and perhaps Archibald MacLeish's *J.B.*, which depended on the story of Job. But again and again the fact rang like a bell in my mind: there is nothing dated about these old biblical stories; they are repeated over and over in human history; they are being acted out right now, all over the world.

Christopher Fry had the trick of it in his play *A Sleep of Prisoners*. The characters were Allied soldiers imprisoned in an old European church during World War Two. As they lay about on the pews and altar of the church and slept, they dreamed a common dream in which they became biblical characters—Cain and Abel, Abraham and Isaac, David and Jonathan,

Shadrach, Meshach, and Abednego. The strange thing was the way their real life characterizations blended with and became those of the biblical personages. With a command of poetry, Fry made his audiences in modern Britain realize that their situation after the war was not at all unlike those of people in other ages. The times change. Jungles give way to cities, and swords become airplanes. But mankind abides. No matter how sophisticated we become, the primitive still lurks inside us. And this is marvelous!

Karl Barth spoke once of "the strange new world within the Bible." It is strange, indeed; strange because we have so seldom entered it. We have carried to the Bible instead our own ideas and philosophies of life and have sought there the corroboration we wanted for those. We have not risked anything by letting the ideas and events there read us.

And it isn't any good, therefore, to complain that the Bible is old, or dull, or eccentric. We have only judged ourselves.

When Thomas Hardy wrote his novel *Jude the Obscure* back at the end of the nineteenth century, it provoked such a storm of criticism everywhere that he never wrote another novel. Nowadays it seems awfully tame, but then it was regarded as a daring attack on the clergy, marriage, sexual morality, faith, the Bible, and a lot of other things the Victorians tended to encircle in sanctity. One of the intellectual currents of the time that was reflected in the novel was the so-called literary criticism of the Bible. Jude Fawley, the central character, was introduced to this phenomenon by his free-thinking cousin Sue, who had a New Testament that had been cut up and rearranged in the supposed chronological order of the composition of its parts. Later, with Sue's help, Jude tore apart a Testament and rearranged it for himself.

Today this seems simple enough. Certainly every seminarian, and even an occasional Sunday school student, knows that the four Gospels were not written in the order in which they stand in the Bible. Mark was probably the first written, and then Luke and Matthew, with John following considerably later. And Paul's letters were probably composed before the earliest Gospels.

But the impact on the religious scene in the nineteenth century was tremendous. What this fact, so obscured for centuries, really meant was that the Bible was not a divinely dictated composition after all, with every paragraph intended just so by God, but a collection of observations and records and exhortations by human beings, a book of impressions by men who were trying to deal with something significant that had happened to them. They had experienced something new and dynamic and exciting, whose first claim was on their manner of living. The writing was incidental to this. And it is important to us for the insight it provides into their thinking and acting under the exquisite pressure of the event itself.

It began to become apparent, in other words, that the New Testament's authority lay not in its self-contained experience for men but in its witness to that experience. And there is an inestimable difference in the two kinds of authority. One made the Scriptures awesome and impeccable, forbidding and magical. The other makes them interesting, lively, and human. One resulted in inflexible orthodoxy and bibliolatry. The other results in exploration and experience. One led to doctrines of infallibility and inerrancy. The other leads to belief and meaning and life.

Let me illustrate the differences this way. Lying on my desk is a letter which my wife wrote me from London. In it she speaks of a telephone conversation we had had a bit earlier, of dinner with some friends, of a visit to the home of some other friends, of how the boys and I were getting along at home, and of a forecast for gale winds on the channel between England and France. The letter was evidently of some importance to me, for it is still lying on my desk several months after its receipt. Now, suppose I had begun to sit around reading this letter all day. Imagine that I began excerpting phrases and sentences from it and scrutinizing them for hidden meanings, that I underlined key words and analyzed verb tenses. Maybe I even began to carry the letter with me everywhere and, to the consternation of friends and associates, to quote it to them at the least provocation. When my wife came home, I was busy reading the letter. She put on her apron and went to the kitchen to make a souffle. I ignored what she was doing—ignored *her,* in fact—because the letter had assumed such an overwhelming importance for me.

Of course, that is not the way it really was. I treasured the letter because it was from her, and I may even have read it more than once. But I did not get hung up on the letter. *She* was the important one, and the letter was only a small clue to her personality, a slight record of some of her many activities.

This is why the modern revolution in thinking about the Bible is so important—it has freed God from the cramped corners we had confined him to! We needn't expect to find out everything about him in the Scriptures. They are only a sometime clue to his nature, his activity, his mystery. They are an important clue, to be sure. They tell us a great deal about him—much more than any of us has yet learned. But they are not the only clue. The world is full of clues. We don't discard the scriptural clue because of that. No detective discards the biggest single clue he has had. But, on the other hand, neither does he cease to look for the other clues and compare them with that one.

The real importance of the Scriptures, then, lies in their witness to something dynamic that happened in the experience of the writers. This is why they spoke of a gospel. Something had happened—something big, something important, something life-changing! It was good news!

Someone told me recently that he was reading a book by the Archbishop of York in which the Archbishop made the statement that all of St. Paul's dogmas were doxologies before they became dogmas. I don't know the name of the book. I don't even know the Archbishop of York. But he must be a pretty wise man to say a thing like that. Dogmas were doxologies before they became dogmas. He is right, you know—and not for St. Paul only, but for the whole New Testament.

We don't know exactly how many songs or parts of songs are imbedded in the New Testament. Scholars are identifying more all the time. Some are easier to recognize than others. There are a number in the first two chapters of the Gospel according to Luke—Luke 1:14–17; Luke 1:32–33 and 35; Luke 1:46–55 (the "Magnificat"); Luke 1:68–79; and Luke 2:29–35 (the "Nunc Dimittis"). The first chapter of the Gospel according to John contains a famous hymn beginning, "In the beginning was the Word, and the Word was with God, and the Word was God." And I heard a scholar say a year or two ago that there is little doubt now that the well-known passage in the second chapter of Paul's letter to the Philippians, the one about Christ's self-emptying to become a man and dwell among us, is really a fragment of an old hymn.

This is exciting to me. Do you realize that these three areas alone—Luke 1 and 2, John 1, and Philippians 2—encompass the most strategic passages in the Bible about the birth and pre-existence of Christ? What must that mean? Could it not mean that the whole matter of Christ's having existed from all eternity and then having been conceived miraculously was for the early church a matter of *song* instead of mere history? If that were so, then it would follow that these passages were never intended to become anvils of doctrine for forging creeds and splitting heads. They were statements of enthusiasm and extravagance, just as songs usually are. They were joyful expressions of the early church's confidence in the Lord who had been taken from among them and crucified by the Romans. They were paeans of exultation.

Bishop Robinson says that the same thing probably happened with regard to the Ascension of Christ. Where did he go if he went up out of sight? To the moon? To another planet? What is "out there" except more space? Of course he was not literally a

[97]

spaceman. But it was necessary for the church to express its absolute belief in the unity of the Son with the Father. He *had* to be with the Father. And for people who lived in a culture which accepted the Ptolemaic world-structure, with the underground and the earth and the heavens stacked on one another like a stack of pancakes, there was no other way to think of his going. They had to think of his going *up*. But again the important thing was not a doctrine of the Ascension, but a doctrine of the reunion of the Son of God (or Son of Man) with the Father.

There is a ten dollar word for this process of getting back to what was really urgent in the Christian message. It is called "demythologizing" (in German it is even worse—*Entmythologieserung!*). As a method of interpreting the Scriptures, it is particularly associated with the teachings of a German professor at the University of Marburg named Rudolph Bultmann. What Professor Bultmann has suggested is that there is a veneer of myth or cultural parochialism associated with first century life and manners of expression which should be peeled away as we attempt to express the same truths in twentieth-century language and modes of thought. Language and thought are dynamic, he says, and change with the times; we cannot even assume that the repetition of the very words of the early Apostles would mean the same thing to our ears that they meant to the ears of their contemporaries. Therefore, it is important to wrestle with imaginal and figurative problems as well as textual problems in making the transition of meaning through nearly twenty centuries.

Feelings run high about such things in some quarters. I know a very dear man who was dismissed from his teaching post in one denominational seminary because he had studied at Marburg and represented the "heretical" ideas of Professor Bultmann. It is a real tragedy that rigidity of interpretation, especially in a matter so open to debate and discussion, should become the rock upon which friendship and fellowship are sacrificed.

Dogmas were doxologies before they were dogmas. That being so, the Virgin Birth and Ascension, whatever the historical facts of the matter, are true *poetically*. That is, they express something profound and otherwise ineffable about the uniqueness of Christ. And that ought to be a sufficient admission for anybody's creed. We are not obligated, as Christians, to be like the Queen in *Alice in Wonderland* and set ourselves to believing half a dozen things that aren't so every morning before breakfast. Our experience is with this Jesus, who set the world on its ear, and that is enough. There need not be conformity of opinion about him or about his miracles or about the nature of the redemption he offers. Jesus—that is the central fact. The rest is embroidery. In him God has shown us MAN again—or maybe man for the first time, if we should discount Adam as a nonhistorical character.

Since that life, men have yearned for him and his image. Even crucifixion didn't stop it. The grandeur of his dying broke over the sordid existence of man like the rainbow spray of the sea crashing upon the rocks. It isn't any wonder that death could not hold him. Something was pulling him, drawing him from beyond. Something? God. This was what the first sermon the world ever heard from a Christian preacher had as its central message. The Nazarene carpenter had been raised from death. Life ought never to be the same again for any man in the world.

"Dear God," wrote one little girl in Eric Marshall and Stuart Hample's *Children's Letters to God*. "Could you write more stories? We have already read all the one you have and begin again."

It is an interesting thought, isn't it? God's coming out of retirement to write some more stories. At least two observations are warranted by this beguiling request. One is that here is another instance of a child's being brought up to believe that the Bible is of exclusively divine composition—"Holy Ghost written," to use an older child's imaginative way of putting it. The other is that maybe there *are* more stories than those contained in the canonized Scriptures. We have already dealt with the matter of the first observation; let's look at the second.

Why are the Scriptures limited to the sixty-six books of the

Bible as we know it? Why those sixty-six books? Why was the recently discovered Gospel according to St. Thomas, for example, not included in the New Testament?

I am not a historian, and will have to give a simplified answer, but it is something like this. The Jews had already fixed the canon (a Greek word meaning "rule" and signifying those books meeting the standards of entry into the accepted Scriptures) of the Old Testament before the time of Christ, and, among the early Christians, to speak of the Scriptures was to speak of the Old Testament; they did not regard their gospel writing and letter writing as an addition to the sacred materials. Several things prompted the writings of Christians after the death of Christ. One was merely the convenience of letter writing as a means of communication—over half of the books of the New Testament were written this way, as messages to persons or churches in other places. Another was the realization, as the years passed and the expected return of Christ did not take place, that the people who had seen Jesus and talked with him were all going to die eventually and should leave some written record of their knowledge of him. We assume that the Gospels, or at least the preliminary accounts behind the Gospels as we know them, were originally composed with this thought in mind.

There were not many close disciples of Christ, but apparently there were many disciples of disciples, and still more disciples of disciples of disciples. So letter writing, and, to some extent, even gospel writing, flourished in the early church. Many churches apparently had "libraries" or collections of letters addressed to them or to individuals among their members. The situation began to become critical after a while, and it became necessary to say which letters or sets of memoirs were most valuable to know and preserve. Different persons held different opinions.

Out of this welter of conflicting theologies and divergent accounts of things emerged the necessity of selecting a corpus of early Christian writings and establishing the priority of that corpus as a determinant of faith and action in the Christian community. Thus the notion of a canon, which had its precedent in the choice of the Jewish Scriptures, arose in the church as a way of dealing with its own literary heritage.

The rule was simple: only those gospels or letters actually written by an apostle or the disciple of an apostle would be included. The application was difficult: who could say, after an interval of more than a century, which works were authentically by an apostle or his disciple? Literary critics are still debating the actual authorship of some of the books of the New Testament. But the church became the possessor of a Bible including the Old Testament—which the first Christians had considered to be the Holy Scriptures—and a number of compositions arising in its own history. For better or worse, the matter was settled.

Canonization of certain writings led, in the Middle Ages, to their being regarded as having uniform value. It remained for men like Luther, who was a biblical scholar before he was a reformer, to remind us that the writings of the Bible are actually of very uneven quality. He called the Book of James "a right strawy epistle" and had little respect for certain other books of the New Testament, notably the book of Revelation, which he found cabalistic and fruitless. The Scriptures, he said, are "the cradle of Christ," and may be judged according to how easily Christ is found in them. This, although it was a relatively simple formula, was the real beginning of a critical philosophy in reading the Scriptures, and subsequent ages have not always done so well in discerning a principle by which to measure the relative values of the various writings.

This is a very unsophisticated and incomplete rehearsal of the history of the canonization of the Scriptures, but perhaps it is enough to suggest that there is nothing intrinsically sacrosanct about the canon and that there may very well have been worthy writings that were not, for one reason or another, included. One may go further, in fact, and say that there is really not any reason why a writing in another century (even our own) might not also be considered valid and "holy." We are not eye-witnesses to the life and ministry of Jesus, and that, from one point of view, is a disadvantage. But it is no reason, if one is a believer in the dynamic life of God in and through the history of man, to disparage the testimony of subsequent generations to that life.

I have known university students, for example, who were far more moved by the *Confessions* of Augustine (5th century) or the *Journal* of George Fox (17th century) or the "pop prayers" of Malcolm Boyd (20th century) than they ever were by the Bible. Who is to say that the Spirit of God is less present in these and other works through the centuries than it is in the canonized Scriptures?

Of course, there are errors of fact and errors of opinion in almost any book or article one reads. But what we've been saying is that the same can also be true of the Bible. We are not talking about composition on two levels, one biblical or sacred and the other nonbiblical or secular. Secularity and sacredness are qualities shared by every attempt at verbal composition. They are invariably mixed in the human situation itself.

The important thing is that God is always being witnessed to by what men write, even when they don't intend it to be so. This is because faith, or the absence of faith, is always saying something about the shape of God in the world. Even a pornographic novel says something about this shape, albeit in a negative way. It says what a pity it is that God has not become more real, more humanizing, in the lives of these particular characters and in their attitudes and behavior toward one another. And when we read a book by C. S. Lewis or Michel Quoist, we are grateful, and realize that the age of faith is not past but continues as long as there are men anywhere who recognize the presence of the Transcendent in our midst, giving order and meaning to our motion.

What is Marshall McLuhan's famous dictum, that the *medium* is the message? The truth of that has dawned on us increasingly, hasn't it? We live in a scramble of words today, a scramble made possible by technology. And we begin to realize that it is not so much the individual words or even individual ideas that are important, but the configurations of words and ideas, the larger patterns of which they are only small parts. The realization of this cannot but have its effect on Christianity, especially as Christianity is a highly verbal and verbalized religion. What it means, essentially, is that we shall pay less and less attention to the minutiae of grammar and particularities of theology, and more and more attention to the constellations of meaning and message in the whole of both Christian and world history. World religions will become increasingly important as ways of understanding our own faith history.

The significance of the Bible will be either diminished or increased, according to how one looks at the matter. For biblicists, who have never held to any book but the Bible and who find it to be the only source of belief and action, it will appear to be a largely forgotten or neglected book; they will propound their either/ors and bemoan the secular world's almost total ignorance of their precious Scriptures. But for others, who appreciate the Bible but do not credit such a radical distinction between the divine and the human, it may seem to become more important than ever, containing as it does the plots for stories the world writes over and over, generation after generation, as though it had never heard them before.

If a man has eyes to see the continuity, I say, and understand that the witness of the Bible is really to a God who is alive in every age, so that none is really more crucial or sacred than another, then he will be more amazed than ever at the high degree of concentration in the old Scriptures, at the remarkable way in which they provide analogues for the most novel of modern experiences. And he will have a far greater sense than the other man of the movement of God through the ages—the movement of the God for whom nothing is ever sacred or secular but in and of itself.

Chapter 5

Living with an Anthropomorphic God

ONE OF THE PROBLEMS with reading the Bible as a human document is that it puts the biblical description of God in jeopardy. This was the concern voiced almost immediately by a lovely woman participating in a discussion of the New Testament as the product of finite authors. "But if the things written there are of human invention," she said, "what assurance do we have that God is like the Bible says he is?" To some people, it is a frightening question indeed.

Obviously, God is not human as we are. Jesus himself is described as having declared that God is a spirit, and that he is to be worshiped everywhere and not in a particular location. But this has never stopped men from describing him in terms of very human attributes. The earlier, more primitive Jews thought of him as being jealous, vengeful, capricious. They spoke of him in what were obviously terms of human anatomy: his eye saw everything, his arm was strong to do what he willed, his heart could be moved, his mouth established his decrees. Later, when the Jewish people themselves were more settled and accustomed to a certain kind of civilization, they began to conceive of the deity in warmer and more responsive ways. Hosea, for example, pictured him as the patient husband who buys his unfaithful wife back from the bondage her immorality has brought her to. And by the first century of our era, Jesus and the rabbis were speaking of God as a father, with all of the nuances of sentiment and meaning stored up in that term.

This was where Freud, who unraveled so much of the mystery of father-son relationships, really grounded his attack on religion. God is only the father we wish we had, he said. He is a dream, a fantasy, an illusion. Failing in our human relationships, we have projected this universal desire for a father onto the clouds and called the result God. And Freud thought he could trace the whole history of belief in God as the history of superstition and fear and loneliness.

It is hardly to be wondered at, in the face of a logical argument like Freud's, that many modern thinkers have regarded belief in God as a hindrance to the maturity of man and have counseled atheism, or at least agnosticism, as a necessary step in the development of humanism. The existentialists in particular have insisted on the abandonment of theology. Jean-Paul Sartre has held firmly to the position he voiced in *Being and Nothingness,* that God is not a meaningful question to modern man. And Albert Camus, who has been the hero of the younger generation for nearly a quarter of a century now, said that belief in God could only inhibit man's realization of his true nature.

But Fyodor Dostoevsky, the tumultuous Russian writer who anticipated most of the arguments and tensions of our century, thought otherwise. He himself went through a period of agnosticism and intellectualism, only to renounce it after the discovery in a Siberian exile camp that life is too deep and wonderful to be explained without God. He saw that God, while he may necessarily be described in terms of human experience, is really the name for the mystery and terror of what is *not* human, for the reality that underlies and encompasses our humanity and that is, because of the finite nature of our vision, always beyond our description and finding out. This is the God whom theologian Paul Tillich in our day called the *ground of being* and the *ultimate reality*. Theologians in the Middle Ages called him the *ens realissimum*—the being with the greatest reality of all.

What is our experience of this God who is more real than we ourselves are? Of course, each of us encounters him in a different way, but here are the accounts of two persons' memories of the experience.

One is the story of a young woman whose life had been particularly stormy. She had been through ten years of agonizing search for a religion she could accept with her whole heart and mind. Her marriage to a Jewish man had particularly inclined her to the study of Judaism. During this period of her search, she had read André Schwarz-Bart's book *Last of the Just*, which is an account of the suffering of the Jews through the ages and, deductively, an argument against the existence of God. She was especially struck by the line spoken by a Jew in a Nazi death camp to another Jew who was comforting his daughter by saying that all their friends were with God. Why, asked the Jew of the father, will you begin that dream again? Was it indeed a dream? She could almost believe so. She had seen how many varieties of human belief in a deity there are. She had searched for something to unify her own thinking, and all she had found was division and divergence of thought.

But that is not all of the story. While she was in the very depths of despair, both in her marriage and in her search for truth, the young woman had an unusual experience. It was what earlier ages referred to as the beatific vision. Only hers was not a vision in the ordinary sense, for she saw nothing with her eyes. She says that she had an overwhelming impression of God as a great, impenetrable wall. That was all it was. But she said it was the most reassuring thing that ever happened to her. Suddenly she realized that God was there, somehow, before all her frantic efforts to probe into his nature. His being was there, confronting her. And she could probe no further. He was real: he was, in fact, reality. All the rest was theory and conjecture. It had some basis in reality, to be sure; but it was terribly limited and partial. God himself was the important thing, and all the other was only fragmentary evidence of his being.

I asked if she had been aware of any words, either spoken in the confrontation or formulated in her mind as a response to it. "Only one sentence," she said. "I kept thinking it over and over: 'God is the living end.' " "The living end" was, of course, a slang phrase for expressing the superlativeness of something in the decade of the fifties. But she had seized upon this popular phrase and transmuted it into an expression with finality and rich emotional content: God was the beyond which there was no other.

The other account of an experience with God was related to me by a close friend as having been told to him by a business-man in the city of Copenhagen. The businessman began his saga in a city in Texas, where as a young man he found himself broke, out of work, and divorced by his wife. While in this triply desperate condition, he received word of a job in Copenhagen which seemed made to measure for him, provided he could get to Denmark. The man was neither a Jew nor a Christian, and was in fact not a religious person at all, but he said that he had the feeling that this job was right for him and that some power beyond himself was going to help him to get there.

His former employment had been as an engineer with an aircraft company, so he went to a pilot he knew and asked for stowage privilege from Texas to New York City. In New York, he sought the same kind of privilege from some pilots who were ferrying a special order of planes to Paris, France, where they were to be picked up by officials from the Saudi Arabian govern-ment, which was purchasing them. This time he was refused. The king of Saudi Arabia had specified that no one except the crews was to set foot in the planes before he received them.

Still the man was not despondent. He went to his hotel room and waited. In a few hours there was a telephone call for him. One of the pilots, with whom he had left his name, was phoning to say that they believed he might be the answer to a dilemma of theirs: they had no one who really understood some of the specialized equipment on the planes and needed someone to explain it to the men to whom the planes would be delivered. Did he know about this particular equipment? As it turned out, the man's work in the aircraft plant in Texas had been on such equipment, and the crews were only too happy to have him accompany them to Paris.

In Paris, the man applied to several car delivery agencies to see if he could not hire on as a driver to take a car to Denmark. At the time, none of the agencies had a car going to Denmark, but one of them knew of a company in Amsterdam that needed a driver to take a vehicle to Copenhagen. A telephone call confirmed this fact. Shortly afterwards, the man ran into an old friend who was piloting a plane from Paris to Amsterdam and was soon on the plane bound for that city, whence he took the car to Copenhagen and claimed the job he had set out to get.

"I am not a Christian," said the man to my friend as they talked, "but I had a sense of the Ultimate guiding me in all of that. And I have always believed in this Ultimate since that occasion."

Two things stand out in both of these experiences. One is the feeling of assurance that God is the ultimate reality behind the ever changing scenery of life which we witness with our human vision; both the woman and the man felt the importance of this reality, and the basically personal or person-oriented nature of it. And the other is the continuing significance, in each case, of having had such an experience; it became a kind of center around which these persons could organize their beliefs and responses to life.

Discovering this center is extremely important to all of us. The failure to find it does much to explain the fragmentedness and loss of humanity which we talked about earlier. Without God, none of our feelings or experiences really has any priority over any other. With him, on the other hand, we begin to move in the world with a new sense of assurance, with new poise and confidence, so that we are really impowered to become what we have it in us to be in life. As one wonderful elderly woman I know has put it, "I do a lot of crazy things that turn out wonderful for me because I know God is in them for me. By any rules of logic, they would be absurd. But with God in them, they always turn out made to order for me."

And how peaceful it is when one believes this! The woman who experienced God as "the living end" still has a difficult life to live. She and her husband are estranged and she is trying to raise two children by herself. But she has learned the real value of what she experienced. She says, "I struggle so desperately at times—and then I realize I'm not alone. I don't have to do it all. God is in on it too."

One of the problems that seems to bother most intelligent people when they think about God is that they are unable to think of him in non-anthropomorphic terms, or terms that don't seem to have been invented anywhere except in our human consciousness. "I have the nagging feeling," said one man, "that the God I imagine is just that—a God I imagine. How can I ever be sure that I and a lot of other people like me haven't just made him up?"

It is a legitimate question. Somehow we are convinced that God must be more—much more—than we are able to conceive of his being, or else not be God.

But actually, this is a problem with everything we know, not just with God. We are simply unable to know anything apart from ourselves as the knowers. What we are, how we think, the equipment we think with, is always involved in the thing we know, not as it is for itself, but as *we* know it. The image we have of things is always *our* image. It does not necessarily

[109]

correspond exactly with the image other people have. Truth is personal, and not merely objective, because we always know it as persons—as persons who are limited in their ability to penetrate, to grasp, to comprehend.

Consider a man's relationship to his wife as an example. He thinks he knows her pretty well. At least he has a *working* knowledge of her—he knows enough about her to live closely with her, to share something of his life with her, to function in the family and in society with her. But then she does something he has not expected her to do—something that shatters or expands his image of her. He is amazed. "You are not the woman I thought I knew," he says. She is and she isn't. She is the woman of whom he had partial knowledge. If he had been more observant, more sensitive, he might have known her better. He could never have known her perfectly.

It is the same with knowing God. We never know him entirely. In fact, we probably know very little about him. What we do know, we know from our own viewpoint, with all its prejudices and limitations. We are simply not equipped to know anything otherwise. To say that we cannot know God apart from a very human way of talking about him is not to say anything about the finiteness of God; it is only to confess that we are ourselves limited and unable to speak of him in any better way.

To a certain extent, we must always *manufacture* the world around us. Not that it isn't there without our being around to experience it. But it is part of our nature as human beings that we have somehow to organize it and name it before we can be comfortable in our relationship to it. An important segment of our education as we grow up is learning the names of things; it is how we orient ourselves in the world. Not that we necessarily understand things better for knowing their names, but we are simply uncomfortable until we do. There is an old joke about Adam's naming the animals. "Lion, hyena, giraffe, monkey, hippopotamus," he announced as they paraded by. "Hippopotamus?" questioned his Maker; "what kind of name is that? Why

did you call that animal a hippopotamus?" "I dunno," replied
Adam, "it just looked like a hippopotamus." You see the point.
We don't feel right about some things until we have had something to do with organizing our relationship to them. And the
result is that all knowledge really involves us, the knowers, fully
as much as it does what is known. We can never withdraw
ourselves and our experience from the picture.

That is why it shouldn't upset us too much to realize that
God, as we know him, is always tainted by anthropomorphism, is
always made in the image of man. We couldn't know him
otherwise, unless it were as a *thing*, with very materialistic
properties like other things we know in the world—and surely
we approximate the truth more by conceiving of him in human qualities than by thinking of him in merely physical
terms.

Philosophers have always tried to avoid either human or physical language about God by speaking of him in abstract terms.
Plato used the word *nous*, or mind. Medieval theologians called
him the *ens realissimum*—the being with the greatest reality
of all. Paul Tillich, a theologian of our own time, used alter-
nately the terms "ultimate being," "ground of being," and "ultimate concern."

But there is no reason to assume that abstractions are better
than other ways of speaking of God. There are times when they
may even be less desirable than human terms, because for some
of us they have less cognitive value than the human terms. They
are clinical, detached, intellectual, and do not permit a full
enough range of emotional response. We acknowledge them
with our heads but do not feel them sufficiently in our hearts.
And this only emphasizes the widely prevalent split between
knowing and feeling which many people suffer from today.

What is really wrong, for example, with speaking of God as
Father, the way Jesus did? It is a word very strongly charged
with subconscious feeling, as Freud pointed out. But is it therefore an improper term? Which is really more capable of express-

[111]

ing a vital relationship, an abstract, objective word or one impacted with emotion and significance? For my own part, there is no word in the history of any language so capable of conveying the wealth and complexity of deep, significant relationship as the word for father. It encompasses so many things—man's physical origin, his lineage, his name, his attributes, his relationship to the race, to history, to all life, all creation, both past and future. More than any other word, this one orients us in time and the universe. Mind, spirit, being are all so vague in comparison!

"There is precisely the trouble," someone will object. "The reason 'father' is not a good word for God is that it is not vague —it is impacted with connotations from our personal experience. If a man's father has been severe or unjust with him, he will tend to conceive of God as a difficult and exacting person. If the father has been a weak man, he may not have a proper respect for the dignity of God. If the Father has been overly Puritanical in his moral views, he may think of God as a kind of moral scorekeeper, tallying up peccadilloes and meting out punishment."

There is, of course, some truth in all of this. It is a valid objection within limits. The trouble is that, in spite of this, there still may not be a better word. There is something about the word, when applied to God, that brings our fullest selves into active participation with the deity. With all our faults, prejudices, and associations, we are summoned forth to an exchange with God. And I question whether any other language can achieve this, whether it can cause us to lay ourselves on the line, with all that we are, the way this word does. I think not. This word allows us to be fully human in dealing with God, and, at the same time that that is the trouble with it, that is also its virtue.

The literature of the Western world, in many of its greatest periods, has displayed an enormous preoccupation with the father problem. Freud named the Oedipus complex after the king in Sophocles' drama. Shakespeare's *Hamlet* really turns on the resolve of the son to be true to the father. The great novels of

Melville and Dostoevsky would not exist apart from the nature of the father problem and their attempt to deal with it. Turgenev even called one of his novels *Fathers and Sons.* Hemingway and Kafka, to name only two major figures in our own century, wrestled constantly with the Oedipal situation. Kafka even wrote a hundred page "Letter to My Father," in which he spoke quite openly of his guilt and frustration in life because he had never been able to please his father. He often thought of committing suicide as a means of reconciling himself to his parent. He never escaped the torture of this remorseful broken relationship.

This is why Freud said religion is an illusion. Troubled in our relationship with the earthly father, we project a super father-figure and worship that; we sublimate our human anxieties into a cosmic deity. And Kafka might seem to be a case in point where this has happened, except that Kafka, so far as we know, remained an agnostic.

But this is specious reasoning. Should we take Freud's word or the word of Jesus? Freud, after all, was a great neurotic himself. It is clear, from Ernest Jones' extremely full biography of him, that many of his conclusions were affected by the beat of his own pulse. And, while Freud performed a monumental service to the study of the mind and how it works, most of his disciples agree today that he was often wrong. Jesus, on the other hand— well, Leslie Weatherhead may have had the last word on that in his book *The Christian Agnostic.* Said he: "If a child who has just learned to play 'The Joyful Peasant' with one hand, criticized Beethoven; if a boy who failed his General Certificate of Education in arithmetic said that Einstein was no mathematician; if a youth, who had just had his verses rejected by the local newspaper, said that Shakespeare had no idea of a sonnet, would we not complain that they had not the necessary equipment to deny? On the lowest level of assessment, Jesus Christ was the greatest religious genius the world has ever known. Suppose that imaginatively we said to him: 'When you were nailed on the

[113]

Cross and said, "Father, into Thy hands I commit my spirit," you were quite wrong. There was no one there. You only wished you had a father. I know better than you. There isn't a God.' Would it not be rather like telling Beethoven that he could not write music, Shakespeare that he was no artist, and Einstein that he had got his sums wrong?"[1]

Freud may have been correct to this extent, that there is a need in all of us for unity with our fathers, and for reconciliation where there is not such unity. Our very natures seem to demand some kind of peace with our origins. This is why the father problem continues to erupt; if there weren't such a need, we would just forget our fathers and go on our way. And it is very often the case that men do not find it possible to live in unity with their earthly fathers.

But this does not invalidate our relating to God as a Father. On the contrary, it may say that we are never really free to be ourselves, to be human—regardless of our relationships to our earthly fathers—until we have discovered this metaphysical relationship with the Father of all beings and are at one with him.

The thing that was so unique about Jesus was his statement —and the obvious fact behind the statement—that "I and the Father are one." That is tremendous! It is overwhelming in its significance. Into a world of troubled and broken relationships —brother against brother, father against son—came a man for whom all relationship was whole. It is little wonder that they said he was born of a virgin—he didn't have a father problem. He and the Father were one; and he had come to make other men one with the Father. It is no wonder they crucified him. They couldn't believe such good news. It sounded like blasphemy.

It is good news, isn't it? That there is a Father beyond fathers, a Parent beyond parents, whose blessing is the most important thing of all in life; that though it is impossible for us to have the

---

[1] Leslie D. Weatherhead, *The Christian Agnostic* (New York: Abingdon Press, 1965), p. 90.

relationship we desire with our earthly fathers, our heavenly Father takes the initiative in repairing our broken relationship to him; that he is the Father in that remarkable parable of the prodigal son, who spent all, including himself, in a far country and then came home to find his parent eager to restore him to sonship and joy; that we can all be reconciled to what is deepest and most meaningful in the universe, and discover our real humanity in the bargain? Good news? There was never any other like it!

Maybe it sounds like wishful thinking to some people. It doesn't to me. And the reason it doesn't is the hundreds of people I know who are full and healthy human beings because of the freedom and release they feel in a relationship to God as their eternal Father. I could have said thousands, because I expect I know that many, but I said hundreds because I don't want the statement to be at all out of proportion to the truth. Even ten would be enough. To see ten men, normal and vigorous, enthusiastic and joyous, over their sense of unity with the Father of all life, would be enough—far more than enough—to convince me of the validity of what they believe. Such persons remind me of the deepest satisfactions of being human.

What should our relationship to God mean to us? That may sound like a terribly presumptious question when we recall that the Westminster Catechism says that man's "chief end" is "to worship God and enjoy him forever." Perhaps what the relationship means to us shouldn't really matter—God, after all, is the important one. But then again, it does matter, according to the Catechism, that we enjoy him; and we probably can't do that apart from what the relationship means to us. So maybe it is not an improper question after all. How do we enjoy God?

There is a clue, perhaps, in the way we enjoy our earthly fathers. When we have a healthy relationship with our earthly fathers, we feel a sense of security, as if things were right between us and our past. It is not just that we feel physically safe—that is an illusion that wanes as we grow older and realize that our parents are not capable of this kind of protection—but that we feel emotionally safe. Call it harmony, peace, serenity, whatever you will. It is as important to us as it is intangible.

And this sense of rightness, of oneness with our fathers, frees us to live our lives. It releases us from the frustrations which arise in those who are in conflict with their origins, who must live always in tension with their backgrounds. It unbinds the energies that were committed to the war between the generations, so that they may be applied more constructively to other affairs.

This was what the bestowal of the blessing meant in ancient Hebrew families. To bless something was to make it full and fruitful; to curse it was to make it narrow and barren. It was important for the son to have his father's blessing. This meant that things stood well between them, that the father's power was passed on to the son.

The same is true in our relation to God. When we have his blessing, signifying that there is harmony between us, we live and act in his power. We feel capable of fulfilling our potential in the world, of being all that we are created to be. We are able to exercise our humanity to its fullest.

If I may use a rather simple illustration, it is a bit like having enough power for a machine to operate properly. The machine may be very sturdy and well constructed. It may be of the most efficient design. But if its source of power is too small, it will not function well. It may whir and rattle as if it were not a good machine at all. It may behave like a very poor machine. But if it is then connected to a larger source of power, it will begin to act like the machine it was made to be. It will hum and purr most pleasantly. It will do its job without apparent effort. The secret, given a good machine, is in the power. Likewise, we human beings do not operate smoothly when our power lags. Even though we are capable of doing better, we seem to be unable to do it. We can't reach the level of our own potential and possibility. But then we make the discovery of a new source of power beyond the one we have been using. Something magical begins to happen to us. We come alive. We do effortlessly the things we formerly did only with great application, if at all. Things seem to fall in place for us. We enjoy life.

And maybe, if we realize that God is our source of strength, we know we are enjoying God. We are enjoying him and worshiping him at the same time, because the enjoyment of our capacities as his creatures is a primary way of acknowledging the importance of the Creator.

I often think of Martin Luther, who is one of my heroes. I like Luther because he was so remarkably earthy at the same time that he was so sensitively religious. The feeling for life and humanity was so strong in him that it would not be curbed by old religious traditions and pieties. It just erupted from the man, finally tearing out the roots of old systems and credos. Luther was a Hercules of a worker. Some people have the notion that he tacked his theses to the church door at Wittenberg and let things take their course from there on. Nothing could be further from the truth. He labored like a man inspired. For days at a time, over a period of years, he hardly emerged from the books and his writings. A complete edition of his papers runs to thousands of pages today. He was preaching and lecturing constantly. His translation of the New Testament did more than any other work to stabilize and determine the course of the German language in modern times. When he was writing or speaking formally, he was surrounded by students and churchmen, all eager to take down his thoughts on this subject and that. And yet, in spite of all this, Luther managed to pray for an hour or two every day. I say he managed to do it. Actually, he prayed *because* he had so much to do. And the more he had to do on a certain day, the more he prayed. He felt that his strength came to him in proportion to the way he was able to submit himself to God, who was the source of the strength. Submission was his way to power.

In the religious manner of speaking, this is called being "in the Spirit." It means that one is operating under the will and influence of God. There is a secularized version of the same phrase. We say, "I'm in the spirit to work today," or "I'm in the spirit for some fun." We say that a musician is in the spirit to produce a piece of fine music, or that a writer is in the spirit to write a poem or a play. And even in this secular sense, we mean that the person is performing his deed at a propitious moment, when he is able to do better than he would at another time; he is taking advantage of the tide, so to speak, and is performing above his normal level. We can understand more easily, because of this secular model, what it really means to be in the spirit of God. It means that one has surrendered himself to the currents flowing over him so that he is, in effect, carried by the currents, borne along, not against his strength, but with his strength, so that his strength is actually carried to a new power. He has, to use Emerson's terminology, made contact with the "oversoul" in the universe, so that he becomes a vehicle for resources beyond himself.

It may be the peculiar tragedy of more sophisticated Christians that we have lost our ability to get into this other gear. We have developed such a fastidiousness, such a reserve, that it is difficult for us to let go and really become channels of divine power. This strikes us as being too naive, too primitive, too bourgeois, for our enlightened era. We don't like to risk our composure by doing anything extravagant or foolish.

It was over against this kind of thinking on my own part that I profited from reading John L. Sherrill's intriguing little book *They Speak with Other Tongues,* which is an account of recent spiritualist phenomena in American religion. Sherrill provided a picture of what Henry Pitt van Dusen once called "the third force in Christendom," standing along with Catholicism and Protestantism—that part of Christendom more concerned with what the early church called "the baptism of the Spirit." Many of the people who comprise this third force come from the lower social strata, but, surprisingly, evidences of the Spirit's baptism, such as the gifts of healing and speaking in tongues, have begun to show up with increasing frequency in more sedate religious groups, particularly in Episcopalianism. Sherrill, an Episcopalian, was himself skeptical of spiritualism when he began writing his book. It was only as he had continued contact with it that he began to see what it really was—not just a form of eccentricity or self-induced hypnosis, though it is always subject to this abuse, but a dimension of spiritual life that is rarely enjoyed by persons who insulate themselves from God by the very forms and traditions by which they profess to seek him.

The important thing in spiritualism is not the manifestations themselves—on tongue-speaking, for instance, St. Paul himself said it is better to speak ten words with sound meaning than a thousand in mere ecstasy—but the sense of abandon and unity with God of which they are but visible evidence. In my own opinion, the ability to speak in a tongue one has never spoken in before, if it is authentic, as many persons claim, might be explained as the release of certain language-storage molecules not yet discovered by our science. We now know that certain molecules do preserve definite characteristics in us from generation to generation, some of these characteristics even lying dormant for ages. It is not out of the range of possibility that some of the molecules should preserve a whole language intact even though several generations of the family which once used it have not been aware of it, and that a moment of spiritual ecstasy should provide the kind of liberation in the depths of the subconscious necessary to bring it to the surface again, for the kind of contact established between the believer and God in the true religious experience is unquestionably a galvanizing occurrence.

We do all kinds of things with such contact that we didn't know we could do. An artist paints a picture and then stands back in amazement. "If I didn't know I was in the studio when this was painted," he says, "I'd swear I didn't have a thing to do with it. It is much better than I am capable of." A minister

[119]

thumbs through a stack of old sermons, preached years ago, and wonders how he did it. "There are insights there," he confesses, "that couldn't have come out of my head." A National League football player makes pious-sounding statements about how God helped him to outrun another player or to catch a difficult pass. "I know he helped me," he says, "because I'm just not that good."

Who can gainsay such statements? Maybe each of these persons had it in him to do the things I've described and just didn't know it. But something had to throw the switch that released the hidden power.

This liberation to be more than our ordinary selves even works for whole families in their life together. I have in mind a wonderful father and mother and five children my wife and I are acquainted with in a New England state. It is a marvelous sort of family, dedicated to the service of others and living all the time in a state of loving excitement. One Christmas they did without Christmas gifts in order to adopt a Vietnamese war orphan. And this is the kind of thing they do normally, without any fanfare, every day of their lives. Whenever we have a letter from them, my wife reads it, pauses for a minute close to tears, and says, "There is still hope for the world." The secret of this family is obvious to anyone who has ever shared a meal with them and clasped hands to pray with them over the food. They live at a level beyond themselves. They live at high tide all the time.

What happens in a case like this? What will explain how the relationship to God is able to work miracles in our lives? We don't know. We only know that it happens.

Sherrill put it this way in the brief introduction to his book. He said he had joined the choir at his church and learned it was a mistake—he just couldn't produce the clear, resonant tones he thought he could produce. Then one night at choir practice he happened to sit opposite a big Irish bass named Bill Brogan, and he noticed that something remarkable happened—he sang better than he ever had before. He commented on this to Bill after the rehearsal. "If that helped," said Bill, "I'll show you something even better next week." The following Thursday, Bill whispered to him, "Lean into me." Sherrill didn't understand. "Put your weight on me," said Bill. Sherrill still didn't understand, but he leaned back until his shoulder blade was resting against Bill's chest. "And suddenly," he said, "I knew what singing was all about. The resonances of his deep voice swelled through my own; effortlessly I made tones I hadn't known were in me." It didn't last long, this moment of virtuosity, but it impressed Sherrill tremendously. What if there is a power beyond us, a God, who whispers to us, "Lean into me"?

We are not bereft of our individuality. Nothing sinks our personalities into a sea where we are all merged and lose our identifies. On the contrary! What is deepest and most real in us is elicited and drawn forth until our truest selves become apparent. And what man, having once had an experience of being his truest self, can ever be content to be less than that again?

Chapter 6

Playing at Worship

A ROMAN CATHOLIC SCHOLAR, Romano Guardini, has said in his book *The Spirit of the Liturgy,* that man, when he is most truly worshiping God, is playing. I find that a singularly attractive idea. It is a real test for the liturgy of the church: does the liturgy really make it more easy, or more difficult, for people to play, to do their thing before God?

The belief behind Guardini's assertion is that it is important for us to be natural when we worship, to be most ourselves when we offer our lives to God. And it goes almost without saying that we are most ourselves when we are at play, when we are caught up both emotionally and physically in what we are engaged at. Even the stuffiest of persons manage to relax somewhat when they are playing, so that their real selves emerge momentarily and have their time in the sun despite the masks of reserve and distance that have been built up through the years.

Most primitive worship proceeded upon the notion that one more or less abandons himself before the altar of his god. I once attended a Samaritan rite for the slaying of the Passover lambs atop Mt. Gerizim. What impressed me most about the entire service was the casualness with which it was done. The families of the priests wandered about inside the sacred area as if they were on a picnic and not about to undertake the most revered action entrusted to the whole religious community. When the lambs were finally slaughtered, the young men went wild with joy, even tossing pieces of entrails through the air to each other. One might think that centuries of performing this same rite would have caused it to become highly stylized and chaste, performed with dignity and severity. But somehow the Samaritans have managed to preserve an almost secular kind of nonchalance and childishness when they do it, probably not greatly different from that of the ancient Jews and Samaritans in their best periods.

Then whence came the idea that we must exercise great restraint on ourselves when we come to worship, and act with unreal dignity and solemnity? Is it not the legacy of some professional priesthood that, wishing to remove the control of worship from the hands of the laity, accomplished this partly by insisting that the act of worship must be done according to the strictest of regulations?

Of course, we do not wish to become over casual in our relationship to God, who is the source of all life and meaning for us. But, precisely because it *is* a relationship that we celebrate, it is important for us to be ourselves when we do it. If we are something less than ourselves, or other than ourselves, we cannot very well be honoring a relationship in which we are principal parties. Guardini is right, rather, that we must come and play before God. We must come and be natural before him, so that we are most truly caught up in the thing we do, and really make an offering of ourselves.

What kind of liturgy, then, is most suited to the importance of our being natural before God?

This is a question of considerable significance in the life of the church today when commissions on worship are busy trying to implement the so-called "liturgical renewal." What baffles me, in all the fuss about liturgical matters, is why most of these commissions appear to be mainly concerned with reviving *ancient* orders of worship instead of discovering radically new ones with merits equivalent to those of the old. Perhaps it is because they realize that the institutional church is one of the staidest organizations on earth, devoted, in many instances, to preserving its reputation for conservatism and slowness-to-change, and are therefore merely giving the church what they believe it will accept. One woman who was on the National Council of Churchs' commission on worship told me that there is no problem in finding artists who are glad to work at contemporary innovations in the church's expression of its devotion to God, but that the real difficulty arises in trying to persuade the church of the importance of such innovations. "The rock we constantly ran aground on," she said, "was the matter of 'good taste.' Everything that was different from what we had always had in the past was accused of being in poor taste. And taste is such a subjective and indefinable thing that we were finally helpless to accomplish anything."

Many of the most sensitive persons of our time, however, believe that ours is a distinctive time, a time different from all other times. Not that they would argue that history does not repeat itself today. But they feel somehow that the extreme violence of the first half of the century, coupled with the technology and superspeed developments of the second half, imparts a radically new character to life in this era. McLuhan's thesis, that the use of television in our age is producing a social and psychological revolution more profound and more sweeping than that inaugurated by the printing press in the fifteenth century, is probably quite sound despite the pyrotechnics of his arguments and presentation. And the crux of the matter, for worship, is whether contemporary man can really worship naturally and completely with liturgies whose locus of origin is in the second and third and sixteenth and seventeenth centuries.

We forget, I am afraid, that the great liturgies invariably grew out of the moods and affairs of the times that produced them. They were organically related to those times. I have read somewhere, for example, that the king of France in Calvin's day sent for some "more of those catchy hymn tunes" that Calvin was using in his services. Today we tend to think of Calvin as being somewhat stodgy and conservative in his notions of worship. But that is because we have, in certain of our traditions, inherited his type of worship with very little modification in the meantime; it has become static and dull and archaic. The fault is not Calvin's, but that of succeeding generations.

It is to our great shame in the church that we have neglected both the impressive poetic means and the tremendous physical and technical means available today for implementing a kind of worship endemic to our times.

Ours has not been an age of great poets, as some ages have been, because we have effectually divorced our poets from the great themes that once made the greatest bards. But it is an age of extremely competent poets, an age when there are perhaps more *good* poets, more sound craftsmen, than there have ever been at one time on the face of the earth. Some of the pieces in small poetry magazines, and even occasionally in a magazine like *The New Yorker,* are incredibly well turned. And, once in a while, such talent is turned toward an effort for the church—an oratorio, an experimental liturgy, a bit of hymnody, a special prayer. When it happens, the effect is dynamic. Suddenly, somewhere, a few people catch the vision of what worship can be like when it is truly contemporary. As one student who had participated in a dramatically new kind of litany told me, "It gnawed loose every rope that was binding me to lethargy and inaction. I was so excited that I couldn't sleep for three days."

It is a pity that we don't have more of such experimentalism.

I remember the first time I attended a jazz mass. The mass itself was no different from other masses in terms of language and order. But all of the music was set to jazz tempo and played by a very effective combo located in the balcony behind the congregation. The first hymn was "All Creatures of Our God and King"—stately, majestic, inspiring—but now with a beat! I watched the people in the congregation. Some patted their feet, some began to sway in time to the music, some nodded their heads. Most of them looked around rather sheepishly at their neighbors at first, grinning apologetically, as if they weren't quite sure they should be enjoying worship so much. But then, when they found that everybody was doing it, they just relaxed and had a good time. The important thing, it seemed to me, was that people were doing something physical as well as mental when they worshiped. Their *bodies* worshiped God. I recalled the image of the old Puritans sitting rigidly through three-hour services in their little churches in New England. Here was something far better—a service in which people worshiped with their whole selves, not just in part. And we know enough about psychosomatics today to appreciate the difference.

Dance itself was of course once a part of the ritual of worship for the Hebrews. King David himself, when the Ark of the Covenant was brought into Jerusalem, joined the celebration by "dancing and making merry" while wearing only a little linen apron. (So 2 Sam. 6:12–15; 1 Chron. 16:27 adds "a robe of fine linen" to his wardrobe.) Dance groups that seek to interpret liturgical and biblical passages by physical movement are thus supported by ancient tradition, although what is really needed is some way in which entire congregations can take part, not merely as observers but as actors.

We suffer today from an over-extension of an admittedly important *Word*-theology. In a day of unusual literacy, when the average adult spends at least five hours a week reading newspapers, magazines, and books and when the radio and television are on for an impressive cumulation of hours each day, we become

[126]

more and more inured to mere words. Sometimes we think we live in a surfeit of words. We long for quietness, for silence, for at least a parsimony of words. And the church's answer has been to pour on more words, to increase the output of printed material, to "out talk" the secular world.

What if we retreated somewhat from this? What if we tried to find more "wholistic" means of expression and attempted to help men find truth through more non-verbal ways?

Sometimes I sit in a high-ceilinged old Gothic building listening to a congregation trying to sing some outmoded hymn to the accompaniment of a wheezing old organ ("Why," asked a young mathematician from Berkeley, "does the church consider the organ such a sacrosanct instrument for religious services?"), and marvel at the disparity between this surrounding and that from which most of the people have come. The businessmen work in contemporary environments, offices with wall-to-wall carpeting, Danish furniture, sleek electronic equipment, and perhaps even piped-in music. The housewives take care of modern houses and apartments with the latest cleaning equipment, and prepare meals in avant-garde kitchens lined with gleaming appliances. Many of these persons have been to the theater or the movies at least once during the week and have sat in plush theater chairs while light and sound were woven into miracles before and around them. Isn't there something strangely anachronistic, I wonder, something out of time and out of place, about what they are doing in the church, as though it didn't even belong to the era in which they live and move and have their beings? Can it really affect their existence at the profoundest level? Can it help them to know themselves in any final sense, and then to offer themselves to the One they are trying to worship? If they succeed in accomplishing what they have come to church for, must it not be in spite of the liturgy and the environment, and not because of them?

I went not long ago to a *mélange* of four plays by Fernando Arrabal, the French-Spanish playwright. The theater was a relatively small one, and the stage was built around all four walls. The audience sat in revolving seats, that could be turned to view the action on any stage at any time. Speakers situated in several parts of the theater introduced sound effects from all directions simultaneously. Lights seemed to flash unexpectedly from any angle, or from all angles at once. As the final play, into which the three briefer ones had been incorporated, built to a climax, the action was going on all around the audience. Light and sound seemed to come from everywhere. The audience was enveloped, as it were, in wrap-around theater. The effect was electric.

As I walked away from the theater afterwards, I pondered about what I had felt there. Why hasn't the church employed "total theater"?, I asked myself. Is the church afraid of being accused of manipulating people? Rubbish! For one thing, there are few churches that have not attempted to manipulate people in one manner or another, though usually they have failed through poor attempts. More important, however, it is entirely possible to utilize such methods legitimately, so that they become vehicles for real response and worship without seducing people out of their senses or violating their true natures.

Unless I am badly mistaken, the only hope for the structured congregational liturgy of the church is for it to take seriously its need for total reconstitution, using both the poetry and technology of our time to supplement and even replace the outdated poetry and poorer technology of earlier times. Until this happens, churches will be filled mainly with persons who attend out of a sense of duty or because of some connection with friends and relatives. And it can only be regarded as dreadfully unfortunate that the most basic and exciting thing in the world, man's relationship to God, should be deadened by a dull and badly mismanaged liturgical service.

I found an example of the unevenness of our approach to the matter when I was in Berlin a few months ago. I entered the strikingly beautiful Kaiser Wilhelm Memorial Church in the square at the end of the Kurfürstendam, which is comprised of the gutted-out tower of the former church, allowed to remain standing as a symbol of the war and the past; a new tower on the eastern side of it; and an octagonally-shaped sanctuary on the western side. The new tower and the sanctuary are constructed of frame-shaped cement blocks enclosing primarily blue glass, with occasional hints of green and violet and other subdued colors. At night, lights from the inside make these buildings glow with soft and lovely radiance amidst the neon signs and other lighting around the busy square. By day, the worshiper in the sanctuary is entranced by the blue light surrounding him and by the long, low altar with the bronze Christ over it, cast so that he appears to be not only crucified but resurrected, both at the same time. I was galvanized by the appearance of this marvelous church building, and wished I could worship there all my life.

Then the hour came for the brief daily service that is held in the sanctuary by the resident congregation. The hymn was an old one, ascribed to Luther. Very fine for its day, its language was somehow strained and stiff in the present situation. The minister's prayers, from an old prayerbook, perhaps in redacted form, were well-phrased and of an admirable cadence. But they were not *our* phrases, not *our* cadence. They belonged to another era. And their presence there, in that gorgeously modern building, stood out like the traditional sore thumb.

If worship does have to do with our relationship to God, then it is vitally important that worship begin by establishing just who we are, of this peculiar time and place, so that when the relationship obtains it will be *our* relationship, and not that of our religious alter-egos, our spiritual masks or *personae*. And who we are is established as much by how we say our piece as by what we say, and as much by the accoutrements with which we surround ourselves as by either how or what we say. If an archaeologist in some long-distant civilization were to uncover one of our church buildings and think it from the period of the

15th-18-century AD, how wrong would he really be? Maybe we are more committed to the past than we are to the present.

At any rate, if worship is to be a part of the living experience of people, it must be of their time. And there is no point in worshiping if it is not a part of living experience. There are the limits of the argument, and we cannot work beyond them.

I sleep better at night when I have prayed before going to bed. Why is that? It is true. When I retire without praying, my life seems still to pulse wildly in all directions, stimulated by many images, and I continue restless when I should be serene and composed. When I pray, however, something peaceful happens. I am at one with myself. All the bonfires on the perimeter of my consciousness go out, and night, calm and restorative, settles on my soul.

I know a gifted young reporter who had a similar experience. He told me that sometimes at night, when he was in graduate school and had been poring over books for hours, the new facts and theories would buzz through his head like a hive of disconsolate bees. Often when it was that way, he said, he would walk over to the university chapel, where students were wont to give recitals on the organ or to be at practice late in the evening, and lie down on a pew in the back. Staring up into the shadowy depths of the vaulted ceiling, he would compose himself for a few minutes and then he would utter a single word: GOD. He said it had a way of clearing his head and bringing all the jumbled and unassorted knowledge into order.

Why? Why is prayer like that? What is there about it that it should result in such peace and tranquility?

There is a lot of confusion about what prayer is, and much of it is based quite simply in our desire to have things. People talk about "answered" and "unanswered" prayer, as if the real criterion for prayer were getting what they asked for. When I was a young minister in a small village, I was told about one man in the town who had stopped coming to church when his daughter

[130]

died. It was said that he had prayed for her to get well, and, when she did not, renounced his faith completely. I knew a young man who prayed for some money, and, when he did not get it, decided that prayer is only a superstition.

Ironically, the words of Jesus, who never prayed for anything for himself but that he might do the will of his Father, are often taken as the legitimation for such acquisitive praying. "Ask and you shall receive." "Whatsoever you ask in my name, it shall be given you." "If you but had the faith of a grain of mustard seed, you would say unto this mountain 'Be thou removed and cast into the sea' and it would be done." But can anyone who knows anything about Jesus' ministry, about his own simplicity of life, about his views on seeking the Kingdom of God ahead of everything else, honestly believe that Jesus was endorsing the making of prayers for selfish social or material ends? It would have been completely out of keeping with his character. Surely, whatever he said about praying and asking was uttered in a uniquely spiritual atmosphere, in a context having to do with the coming of the Kingdom and not in one oriented toward the mere acquisition of what men desired for themselves.

When Jesus himself prayed, it was generally for continued union with the Father. If his day was a busy one, he withdrew, sometimes before it began, sometimes during the course of it, to pray. Prayer, for him, was communion more than anything else. Of course he prayed for specific things too, and advised the disciples to do likewise. But communion came first; it was the ground of all other prayer.

This is what many people have forgotten. Prayer is not an ordering service with a divine bellhop at the other end. It is communion. It is God's sharing time, when we wait in his presence and have our thoughts and desires reordered, when we are united to him and his work in the world, when we are restored to him and he receives us in our brokenness and spentness. This is why we sleep better at night when we have prayed, or work better in the day, or think more clearly about our studies, or perceive more about life—because we have been reunited to the center of all existence and have felt new order and vision transmitted to our own persons.

Malcolm Boyd's discovery of this resulted in the meaningful little prayers of *Are You Running with Me, Jesus?*, which assume, prior to their composition, that being in touch with God is important to every secular task and sensation we have. "Prayer, for me," says Boyd, "used to stand as something separate from other parts of life. But I have come to learn that real prayer is not so much talking to God as just sharing his presence. More and more, prayer and my style of life as a Christian now seem inseparable."[1] This is the way it ought to be in every man's life. Prayer should seem so indispensable in discovering what is unique, what is different, what is exciting about him personally that he would deem it inseparable from his style of life. It is not something tacked on to his existence, like the tail of a kite, but something integral to it, something so important to it that it cannot be neglected without great loss.

I once heard a housewife describe prayer as a kind of vacuum in her day that drew her inward into her real nature and real self. She said that she believes every person feels such a pull upon him from time to time but that many people don't recognize what it is. Some women, when they feel it, answer by going on a shopping spree. Some people answer it by having a couple of drinks. "If only they realized what the right response to that urge could mean to them," said the housewife. It was obvious that this was one of the greatest sources of joy and radiance in her life.

Leslie Weatherhead, in *The Christian Agnostic*, cites Florence Allshorn's piquant little prayer, "O God, here am I and here are you." If only more people prayed like that, what a difference it would make in their attitudes toward prayer. One can sense immediately the air of inwardness, of casualness, of

---

[1] Malcolm Boyd, *Are You Running with Me, Jesus?* (Holt, Rinehart and Winston, 1965).

resignation in it. How it would change our lives if we prayed it sincerely every day! Just to repose ourselves before God, to loosen our ties and undo our shoelaces and say, "Well, here we are, you and I; it's good to be with you again."

Do you remember Jesus' prayer for his disciples? It was mainly concerned for the union of their existence with God's— and for *ours:* "Neither for these only do I pray, but for them also that believe on me through their word; that they may all be one; even as thou, Father, art in me, and I in thee, that they may also be in us: that the world may believe that thou didst send me. And the glory which thou hast given me I have given unto them; that they may be one, even as we are one; I in them, and thou in me, that they may be perfected into one; that the world may know that thou didst send me, and lovedst them, even as thou lovedst me" (John 17: 20–23, ASV).

Doesn't it follow that our praying ought to be for the same thing? Shouldn't an identical concern guide us and orient us, so that we offer ourselves to it and make a similar prayer for other persons we know?

Here is a passage from Michel Quoist's impressive little book *Prayers of Life,* simply entitled "My Friend":

I shook hands with my friend, Lord,
And suddenly when I saw his sad and anxious face, I feared that you were not in his heart.
I am troubled as I am before a closed tabernacle when there is no light to show that you are there.
If you were not there, Lord, my friend and I would be separated.
For his hand in mine would be only flesh in flesh
And his love for me that of man for man.
I want your life for him as well as for me.
For it is only in you that he can be my brother.[2]

Isn't this what prayer is really about? About enlarging the di-mensions of the soul, about being united, truly, deeply united,

---

[2] Quoist, *Op. cit.,* p. 17.

with other persons in God's world, about feeling and sensing and loving in that world? In short, about being more human?

Some people think of prayer as a kind of pious activity they can do without. That may be true of certain kinds of prayer—mere recitations of phrases or requests for selfish ends. But it is not true of this kind of prayer. On the contrary, no man anywhere, whoever he is, can really afford to miss out on this kind of praying, for to miss out on this is to miss out on being a fuller and more sensitive human being.

It is not an easy kind of praying—at first—for it involves a journey inward, and inward journeys are always the hardest. Other kinds of praying are much less exacting, ask less of the one praying. But in the end it is the *only* way of praying, for it is the only way that holds the one praying and what is prayed for in tension, so that the world is genuinely changed.

Prayer delivers the world to me, because prayer delivers me to the world.

Chapter 7

Making the Most of Conflict

No MATTER HOW CLOSE to God we are, or how effective our prayers are, however, we must still face conflict in the world.

That is bothersome to some persons, though it oughtn't to be. If God is good, their argument always runs, and God is all-powerful, then why does he permit men to suffer? Why does he permit little children to die of hunger in India and China or disease in France and America? Why does he permit poverty and illiteracy and misunderstanding? Why does he permit idiocy and neuroses and nervous disorders? Why? Why? Why? Maybe we have got to face the fact that he is not all-powerful—at least not in any sweeping way. Maybe we have yet to see that he is in us and with us, working through us and not apart from us, limited by what we are, by our weaknesses and our unwillingness. Maybe we have yet to understand that goodness and rightness have a might with a qualitative difference from the force which disease and hunger and death wields against us, so that their victory is a long and arduously won thing and not a swift and effortless one.

[135]

Jesus himself was not immune to suffering; his passion was in fact so much the epitome of human suffering that it has become the central image of it in art and literature. Saint Paul said he prayed for years for the removal of a "thorn" in his flesh. We aren't sure what it was—recurrent malaria, perhaps, or possibly even a moral problem. But it was never removed, as far as we know; the answer he had in prayer was that God's grace was sufficient for him. Most of the early Christians were faced with the constant threat of torture or death. Much of the literature which circulated among the churches in their day contained messages of encouragement about this, reminders that suffering purifies and that it is not to be compared to the worth of the life the Christian is striving for. Why should we, who are eminently more comfortable than they, complain about the presence of evil and suffering in the world?

There is a tremendous sense of conflict in the world today—sometimes amounting to a general feeling that the powers of darkness are almost insuperable. Complaints against the injustice of man's position have been voiced in modern literature since the days of Melville, whose posthumously published *Billy Budd* is the story of an innocent young sailor who was put to death by his ship's captain to preserve order among the other sailors. Some critics think the captain represents God in the story and that Melville was raising his fist against the Creator of a universe where innocence suffers and evil appears to triumph. Whether Melville intended this meaning or not, there is a whole generation of young people who would contend that this is the way it is, that authority, wherever it is, is in conspiracy against all the individuals in the world who want to live in peace and innocence. Hence, they have become "permanent revolutionaries," waging war against the established order regardless of what it is or stands for. The result is that ours is, in many ways, the most cynical age in recent history. Many people are bitter because they cannot understand how a deity who is supposed to love everybody can tolerate such an unjust universe; or else they must conclude that there simply isn't a deity.

Somerset Maugham, the writer, said in *The Summing Up* that, contrary to the view that suffering ennobles people, it had been his experience that it only makes them mean.

I have thought about that statement for a number of years and have decided that I cannot agree with it. As a sometime minister, I have known many people's misery. There have been times, in fact, when my wife and I would shake our heads and wonder how men can bear so much. But I have not found that suffering makes people mean. To the contrary, I have found that it often makes them sensitive, thoughtful, and considerate of others. When I meet someone who appears to be very compassionate, my first guess is always that he has suffered a great deal in his lifetime.

When we lived in New England, I used to visit a woman who was ninety years old. When she was younger, she had been a midwife and had delivered hundreds of children, both in England, which was her former home, and in New England. She had reared a large family of her own. Now she was crippled by arthritis and afflicted by a glandular disease that made it impossible for her to move about. Her days were spent in bed and in a wheelchair, and she never left the single room on the top floor of the old farmhouse where she lived. Her pain seemed nearly unendurable; her daughter-in-law, who cared for her, said that often she cried out in her sleep, when she could not consciously restrain herself. But she was not bitter about it. She was far more concerned about other people's pains and burdens than she was about her own. Far from resigning from the world because of her affliction, she knew more about her neighborhood than anybody else. She sat for hours at a time watching the children come and go, seeing the first winter snowfall, spotting the first crocus that popped into view in the Spring. And sometimes when she described to me some sight that particularly touched

[137]

her, like that of a little boy who followed his mother around as she planted flowers and picked all of them as fast as she set them out, her eyes would become luminous with tears and she would say how wonderful life is. Her life wasn't what it had once been, when she was healthy and active, but she was holding onto what there was, for it was dear to her. I never once came away from a visit with her up in that room overlooking the world that I didn't feel richer, happier, and more in love with my own life.

When I was a college teacher working with undergraduates, I knew a paraplegic boy who spent his entire academic career in a wheelchair. Another boy was paid an allowance to live with him as his roommate and see that he got to all of his classes. When the handicapped boy graduated, the entire audience at the commencement exercises gave him a standing ovation. Years afterward, the young man who had been his constant companion and helper told that the experience of living with that boy was the finest thing that had ever happened to him. He said, "I never have a difficulty now without remembering how he never did anything without the extremest difficulty. And when I recall how he took it, how he never complained about anything, how he just went ahead and did what had to be done, even when it hurt him to do it, I thank God for the ability to get up and dress myself in the morning and I feel ashamed for every complaint I ever made."

Of course, both of these persons were individuals who had a great faith in God and the ultimate meaning of life. Maybe the people Maugham knew were different. But one's *attitude* toward suffering is doubtless a decisive factor in how it affects him.

The Hindu philosopher Tagore, whom I have mentioned previously, felt that way. He told a story once about a game which a little girl played with him. She asked him to imagine that he was shut up in a room that had been locked from the outside and to tell her how he was going to get out. He said that he would call for help. But she was not willing for him to get out so easily; she promptly replied that all help had been removed from the area. He said then that he would kick the door down. She promptly made the door into a steel one. Each time he proposed some solution to his dilemma, she invented some additional impediment to his escape. Thus it is in life. There are times when we are blocked at every turn. Whatever solution we devise to our problems, we come immediately upon some new difficulty. How a man accepts difficulty, then, becomes all-important. If a man is cowardly and complains all the time about his lot in life, he has chosen one way of living. But he need not choose this way. He can regard conflict as a natural part of existence and meet it with resolution and ingenuity. Suffering can become a spur to creativity.

One has but to recall Milton's blindness, Beethoven's deafness, Coleridge's headaches, to remember what grandeur humanity has often achieved in spite of difficulties. Dostoevsky, who spent several years in the lonely exile of Siberia before becoming a great novelist, said that "suffering is the sole origin of human consciousness." Suffering, unless we abjure it and retreat from it, causes us to sharpen our wits, discipline our talents, and develop our possibilities.

It may be argued, of course, that the examples I have used are those of persons with severe physical handicaps, and that there are other kinds of suffering harder to deal with because they are less tangible. What of the parents of a retarded child in those difficult years when they are in the process of accepting their child's handicap and learning to handle it? What of the longsuffering wife of a man who refuses to get a steady job and support his family? What of the man who is hag-ridden by fears of every kind and cannot lead a normal life because he is afraid? What of the person who is simply "burned out" on his fellow human beings because he has not found cause to trust any of them? These are surely modes of distress not uncommon among us, and ones that are extremely hard to cope with.

But again, it is true in every instance that one's attitude makes a world of difference in the problem he is facing.

[139]

Viktor Frankl, the psychotherapist, devotes a considerable portion of his book *Man's Search for Meaning* to the similarity of the importance of attitude among prisoners of war both during their confinement and in their lives after the war. It was easy enough to document this importance in the prison camp itself.

"We who live in concentration camps," he said, "can remember the men who walked through the huts comforting others, giving away their last piece of bread. They may have been few in number, but they offer sufficient proof that everything can be taken from a man but one thing: the last of the human freedoms —to choose one's attitude in any given set of circumstances, to choose one's own way."[1]

After the war, the identification of the significance of attitude was not always so simple. Men who had stayed alive because of their dream of the future were suddenly plunged into that future, which had become the present, and found it less rewarding than they had expected. Some returned to their villages to tell of their hardships but were met only with shrugs and the reminder that it was a difficult time for everybody. Some stood before the homes they had longed to go back to and stared only at the charred remains of their former houses. Some rang the doorbells they had waited so long to ring and found total strangers living there. Some found their wives remarried, their children distant and suspicious. The predictable suffering of the prison camps was much more readily handled than this. Besides, it had been obviously shared by countless others. Here was a new, intense kind of suffering felt keenly by men who thought themselves past all suffering—and it bore with it an overpowering sense of loneliness, of being set apart and isolated in the experience. It was more like the suffering individuals meet all the time in their lives.

Frankl apparently did not have the opportunity of following up the cases of men who did go home from the death camps to

---

[1] Viktor, Frankl, *Man's Search for Meaning* (New York: Washington Square Press, 1963), p. 104.

such problems, but he cites enough illustrations of the more common situations to convince us that attitude must have played the major role again in these. He tells, for example, of a doctor who lost his wife and, two years later, still complained of severe depression. What could a therapist say? Frankl asked him what would have happened if he had died first and his wife had survived him. "Oh," said the man, "for her this would have been terrible; how she would have suffered!" Whereupon Frankl replied: "You see, Doctor, such a suffering has been spared her, and it is you who have spared her this suffering; but now, you have to pay for it by surviving and mourning her."[2] The man had never thought of it in that light. Quietly he shook the therapist's hand and left. Somehow suffering begins to lose its grip on us once we have discovered some meaning for it, or have amended our attitudes so that it cannot destroy us.

I have always been struck by what is revealed about suffering in Theodore Dreiser's last novel *The Bulwark*. Dreiser had been waiting for years to get back at his father, who was a poor evangelist in a midwestern city, for his memories of the old man's piety and poverty, and he thought he would do it in this novel by picturing the novel's hero, a Quaker named Solon Barnes, breaking down under a series of calamities. But as Dreiser "researched" the book and became more and more familiar with Quaker beliefs and history, something began to happen to him. He realized that the traits he had endowed Solon Barnes with at the beginning of the novel—gentleness, honesty, faith in his relationship to God—would not really permit Solon to go to pieces. If he was to be true to his craft of fiction, and follow the inner laws of character to their natural consequences, he must represent Solon as emerging quietly victorious over his many afflictions. Dreiser was so thoroughly impressed by this that it had an effect on his own life and thinking. He began to attend church, irregularly, and to seek some of Solon's strength for his

---

[2] Frankl, *Ibid.*

own existence. And finally, before he died, the old despiser of religion even received Communion. He was convinced that a man who believes deeply, who has a relationship to the source of life, suffers better than one who does not.

The final paradigm in this matter of belief and suffering is of course that of Jesus on the Cross, who uttered both the Cry of Dereliction, "My God, my God, why hast thou forsaken me?" and the Saying of Affirmation, "Father, into thy hands I commend my spirit." The Cry of Dereliction is a marvelous study in the complexity and ambivalence of the human spirit. A line from the beginning of the 22nd Psalm, it obviously expresses a sense of great anguish and separation from the deity; it is the sort of thing a man utters in a moment of great pain or despair. But the balance of the psalm, which Jesus undoubtedly knew as well as he knew the lines in his own hand, is not a mere *cri de coeur,* not a testament of isolation, but a strong expression of faith in God, a testimony that God will not leave the deserted one alone but will save him from the evil that has befallen him. This does not mean, of course, that the cry from Jesus' lips was any less human, any less anguished; it was a real cry of hurt, wrung from the soul of a man wracked by pain. But it does mean that the cry was not entirely one of desolation, that it contained the irony of the human situation in any age, for, at the same time that it bespoke agony of soul, it bore the weight of the poetry which followed it as an affirmation of God's care and intervention. He both was and was not deserted. In his brokenness, he felt that he was; in his heart, he knew that he was not. Thus, when the crest of the pain had passed and he knew how things were, he went to death with the words, "Father, into thy hands. . . ." There was no breach; there was only union.

Sometimes it is in accepting difficulties or overcoming handicaps that we discover the most essential part of our humanity. Life is glorious, like the shining sea; but, like the sea, it is most beautiful where the rocks and barriers turn it back in an iridescent spray of foam or mist. Snug little harbors and lazy lagoons are fine enough in their way; but there is something that desires a clash and a wildness too. Then, in the moment of conflict, the "boredom of living" gives way to the "suffering of being."

There is one conflict from which none of us emerges, at least not in this life, and that is death. Therefore, death holds a peculiarly frightening mien for many persons, and apprehension regarding it influences our existence in numberless ways.

A minister once told me of a man in his congregation who thought constantly of death and was convinced, though he was a comparatively young man, that he was going to die within the rather obscure but somewhat proximate future. He had already purchased his cemetery plot and had picked out a tombstone to his liking. He had written down instructions for the minister about how his funeral was to be conducted. He had arranged for far more insurance than his median-range salary could really afford. He had talked about his passing so long and so incessantly that his family was really quite tired of the subject. His teen-aged son had been heard to say, on more than one occasion, "Dad's riding his hearse again." Apparently, the man had become so totally obsessed by the thought of dying that he was basically incapacitated for living. Yet he was physically healthy and probably capable of living for many years.

Again, it is the meaning one attaches to the phenomenon of death that determines part of its significance in his case. One cannot always forestall death, or avoid it, by the attitude he has toward it, but the attitude is extremely important in shaping the life of the one who must someday die.

It would be foolish to ignore the monstrousness of death. There is a finality about it, in terms of our relationships in this world, that no amount of spirituality, either in religious or purely spiritualistic terms, can ever succeed in mitigating. It means a wrenching apart of a man from the growing lives of those he loves, from the environment where he feels at home. And it means a vacancy in the existence of those who are left behind.

I will never forget an evening my wife and I spent with a dear Christian lady whose husband had died several years before. She set a place at the table for him just as if he were present for the meal. She did not talk to him or anything like that. She just honored the great emptiness she felt where the relationship had been.

Another time I blundered by inquiring of a couple of older folks, whom I knew to have had a daughter, as to where she was living. "Our daughter is dead," one of them said. My wife nudged me, but I continued. "That is sad," I said, "but I am sure you are grateful that you had her for the time you did." "Yes," they replied, "she was a wonderful girl. She never gave us a minute's trouble. We love to think of her. But of course we miss her very much. She would have been thirty-nine this year, and we cannot help wondering what it would have been like if she could have lived and raised her family."

So there are realities of separation and loneliness that cannot be dodged, no matter what one's view of death.

Still, one's attitude is very important. Some persons, like the man I mentioned a bit earlier, live in such constant fear of mortality that death begins to dominate them long before they are actually ready to die. They lament, like Bérenger in Ionesco's play *Exit the King*, "Why was I born if it was not forever?" Every ache or pain, every gray hair, every wrinkle, becomes a trumpet of doom. They feel their pulses every hour and wonder if it will be the last.

How much healthier, by contrast, seems the attitude of a man like Stephen Leacock, the Canadian economist and humorist, who, when told that he was facing death by cancer, replied, "Well, if that is the case, give me a stick and I will face it." Here was a case where personality continued to assert itself even at the edge of the abyss. There was no cowering or cringing. There was just the acceptance of this reality that must come, one time or another, as part of the human situation. He had never allowed it to cast its shadow over the rest of his life, however; he held it to the minimum of its power.

It is folly to permit death to take away anything from life; that is giving it more than its due.

A proper sense of death, on the contrary, ought to make life more meaningful. The realization that the lights are going to be turned out should make us scurry to fulfill our duties and desires before it happens. I am all for the Christian interpretation of death that sees it as the passage to a still more wonderful existence, *if,* but only if, it provides the feeling of security that enables one to live more fully and joyfully in this world. In this respect, no one possesses the earth quite like a saint. But I am strongly opposed to such a view if it results in a state of suspended animation, so that the person only postpones living until he finds himself in another world.

A young Catholic girl sat in our living room one evening and talked about faith and life. She said that one of the most vivid memories of her life was an old nun she had once seen sitting on a bench "just waiting to die." She had seen it when she was only a child, but the vision had never left her. Somehow she thought she had sensed the desperation in the old woman for having lived her life in a rather narrow kind of religious devotion and awakened from it too late to do anything about it. The girl was determined that she should not come to the end of life with the same kind of regrets.

Life is of God, and it is meant to be lived. There is surely no greater crime, no greater sin, than to cramp it and confine it so that it has little opportunity to be enjoyed.

If one really lives his life, on the other hand, lives it fully and freely, so that he senses the innate goodness and meaning of it, then death is not something terrible and horrible but a natural and fitting part of experience. As the Upanishad says, when one realizes his Person, he does not suffer from death. Death does not really destroy him or what he has stood for; it only brings to a close this segment of his existence.

[145]

I used to think that it was extremely important, if one was to live unafraid of death, to believe in the life beyond death as something totally separate and distinct from the life we live now; but the older I get the less I am sure of this. It may be that there are only thin boundaries between this world and another tremulous, more spiritual one, and that those who are crossing over, as Leslie Weatherhead maintains, receive a vision of what lies ahead and become eager to embrace it. I don't know. What I do know is that I don't do nearly enough to fill up the life I have, to exhaust the wonder and beauty of the world that is already mine. Why should I want to pile inanity upon inanity and build an eternity out of that? I have an eternity of possibilities in my grasp right now, and I must look to the realization of those.

As for the rest, I am quite prepared to trust God. The sense of relationship I feel to him and the rest of the world, when I am at my best and most alert, readies me to accept whatever dispensation is made beyond this present one. What I feel now is good, I know, and that conditions me not to be ill disposed toward what is to come. I am willing to say, with the rankest fundamentalist, that God is God over death, that he has mortally wounded it, and that he will achieve final victory over it. I do not doubt that for one moment, for I am able to experience, in my own mind and heart, the real and present peace that proceeds from that belief. If I do not choose to spell out the nature and details of what is to come beyond the moment of death, it is because I am eminently satisfied with the potential of life on the earth now, and because I am convinced that I have absolutely no power to see beyond it.

Life is all conflict; that is its nature. But our *life,* our real life, arises from the friction, from the experience of it. Without suffering, without opposition, we should not be able to appreciate it at all, we should not know joy. And mortality, as the final form of conflict, is part of the strange beauty of all that lives— the fragile flower, the faded painting, the worn grave stone, the life with hues of sunset striking its chiselled planes. It is not

hard, if one has the proper attitude, to "go bravely into that dark night."

Whether life is or is not worth living, said Albert Camus, amounts to the very first question of philosophy; all the other questions either come afterward or are not worth asking. And if life *is* worth living, then joy ought to come from just being alive. Camus thought so. Meursault, the character in his novel *The Stranger,* says that he could live forever imprisoned in a tree trunk if only he could see the sky above.

I have never ceased to be impressed by a letter I once read that was written by a German prisoner of war to his family at Christmas time. He described the conditions of his imprisonment, and then talked at length of his memories of Christmas at home—of the candlelit tree, the singing, the exchange of gifts, the walk in the woods on Christmas Day. On the last Christmas they had all seen a deer in the forest. Now there was no certainty that he would ever see his family again. But in spite of this he was able to write: "I feel a strange joy where I am, as though all things were right. I hope you are not suffering, as I am not. I do miss you, and know I am missed. But we have so much to be grateful for!"

There is every evidence that joy can persist thus under the most adverse conditions and is not dependent on a more superficial kind of welfare. Thinking of Christmas, I am reminded of a man who died in my parish once just a few days before the holidays. He had been ill for many years and was in and out of the hospital frequently. The first words his wife said when I arrived at the house were, "I am so happy. I don't know what I will do without him, but I am so happy. He won't suffer any more." Her eyes and cheeks were glossed by tears, but, even in her sorrow, she was glad. And I recall the visage of the man in the hospital—I did not even know his name—who had just been told that his wife had died. "This too is life," he said. I have thought of those words many times. Somehow, joy arises from loss and suffering and toil as much as it does from pleasure and ease. It is much deeper than the surface of existence; it has to do with the whole structure of life. It is the perfume of the rose that is crushed, the flash of color in the bird that is hit, the lump in the throat of the man who sees and knows, instinctively, that life is a many-splendored thing.

The intuition of joy can reach us in so many different ways. In Dostoevsky's novel *The Brothers Karamazov*, Dmitri Karamazov, who is on trial for his father's murder, feels it when he awakens from a deep sleep and finds that someone, he doesn't know who, has placed a pillow beneath his head. This little deed of kindness in a time of such distress has a remarkable effect on him. He knows, if he never realized it before, that there is great good in life along with the evil and misfortune. And this knowledge prepares him to endure any hardship, for it is all a man needs in life.

My wife and I experienced such a joy one day when we had been depressed by news of illness from loved ones and by our own sense of exhaustion. The doorbell rang. It was a young man who worked as an assistant to the custodian in the apartment building where we were living. He was an extremely poor young man, with a family to support and a meager income, and he did not speak our language very well. But he had brought a gift of two homemade donuts for our children and presented them as if they had been royal treasures. Somehow, this act dispelled our gloom and made us very happy. Life did not seem nearly so foreboding as it had.

On another occasion, I was feeling somewhat low because of the pressure of my work and the number of counseling cases with which I had recently dealt. Literally everybody seemed to have an insurmountable problem. How terrible and unrelenting life is, I thought; all of my friends are suffering so. But then I happened to hear my seven-year-old son Eric coming down the hall singing the Doxology. He had never sung it before, but he had been attending church regularly in recent weeks and had shown an inordinate interest, for one so young, in all the parts of the service. Now, in his small voice, a bit unsure in places, he was singing, "Praise God from whom all blessings flow." I was suddenly moved—so much so that tears formed in my eyes. It was just what I needed. I squared my shoulders and knew I could go on—forever, if necessary.

Why is this? What is the emotion we call joy, that it springs from such occasions? What, indeed, but an insight, through some deed or word or object, as through a tube or hole, into the very core of being, the very heart of all existence, in which one descries that all things cohere in a kind of basic goodness. It is only a glimpse, rarely more; the nature of things is such that we cannot see more at one time. But it is enough to persuade us that the universe is not all unjust and unfeeling and irrational, and that is all that is necessary.

When I was in a foreign country once, I had to undergo an operation. The days immediately prior to it were extremely painful ones, and my mind and body were considerably worn by the ordeal. I felt terribly alone, entering a hospital in another land to be served by a physician who did not speak my language. On the morning of the day I was to enter the hospital, my wife attended church. She saw there a friend of ours who was a native of the country. "Tell John," he said to her, "that I am holding him in my prayers." I was standing at the bathroom sink when she told me, combing my hair. The impact of the words, in my nervous condition, was overpowering, and I burst into tears. I felt deliriously happy. To think he was praying for me. Somehow I was no longer alone. I was not far from home; *this* place was my home; *any* place would have been my home. I knew that then. I had seen to the heart of things.

"Joy," wrote André Gide in his diary. "Joy . . . I know that the secret of your Gospel, Lord, lies altogether in this divine word: Joy." And Gide was right. That was how the angels announced the birth of Christ—as "tidings of great joy."

Significantly, suffering and pain did not stop at that moment.

The Massacre of the Innocents—Herod's slaughtering of the male babies under two years of age—occurred shortly thereafter. The Incarnation could not be explained as a release from human problems. It had to be seen instead in terms of insight—insight of the kind we have been talking about. God was with us, said the angels—with us in the problems. Outwardly, nothing was changed by the coming of Jesus. But inwardly, we were made aware of something we had not been sure of—that there is meaning and purpose in life, that there is God, that life is good, that suffering cannot begin to touch these things.

That is why the saints of the New Testament era went so gladly to death—as though "smelling it afar off like a field of flowers," said Chesterton—because they had seen the essential rightness of the universe and were unafraid. It was to the Christians at Rome, where persecution was apt to be quickest and most severe, that Paul wrote his diapason passage, "Who shall separate us from the love of Christ? Shall tribulation, or distress, or persecution, or famine, or nakedness, or peril, or sword? As it is written, 'For thy sake we are killed all the day long; we are accounted as sheep for the slaughter.' Nay, in all these things we are more than conquerors through him that loved us. For I am persuaded, that neither death, nor life, nor angels, nor principalities, nor powers, nor things present, nor things to come, nor height, nor depth, nor any other creature, shall be able to separate us from the love of God, which is in Christ Jesus our Lord."

If this is so—if joy is the product of seeing that there is meaning and goodness in life—then why isn't our joy more full? Why is it limited to a few occasions when some particularly touching occurrence affects us at the depths? Why can't we actually live in joy?

We should, of course. Life was made for joy, and there is an eternity in every instant of it.

Most of us, though, are like men who live in a prison and only get outside it occasionally. When we do get out, when we escape from the stuffy cells where we spend most of our lives, we are so unaccustomed to the new surroundings that we are fairly overwhelmed by them and cannot absorb the impressions that come to us. The child does not yet live in such a prison. The world for him is still quick with magic and discovery, and he is yet capable of ecstasy. Ecstasy seems no strange thing to him. But society— his parents and relatives, his teachers and older associates—soon begin building his prison walls for him, and work hard at it until he is old enough to take over the job for himself and continue what they have begun. And then one day he is no longer free. The prison is finished, and he will get outside of it only occasionally in his lifetime. The impressions of life he receives from then on are mostly routine. Life seems heavy and dark and methodical. Gone are the lightness and effervescence and adventure.

How we ought to pray, then, for delivery from our gray prisons! How we ought to scheme to get outside the walls we have built, beyond our habitual responses to everything, and see the world again. I wonder what it would all be like to see it fresh and new again, without the blinders I have worn so long. Surely I would blink and gape at the miracle of it, and pinch myself to see if I were dreaming or not. How marvelous it would be!

Frankl has recorded in his book how he felt as he entered the world again after years in a concentration camp. "I walked through the country past flowering meadows," he said, "for miles and miles, toward the market town near the camp. Larks rose to the sky and I could hear their joyous song. There was no one to be seen for miles around; there was nothing but the wide earth and sky and the larks' jubilation and the freedom of space. I stopped, looked around, and up to the sky—and then I went down on my knees. At that moment there was very little I knew of myself or of the world—I had but one sentence in mind—always the same: 'I called to the Lord from my narrow prison and He answered me in the freedom of space.' "[3]

---

[3] Frankl, *Ibid.*, pp. 141–142.

Most of us would have similar emotions on reentering the world from our own self-made prisons—on discovering that we are really surrounded by "the freedom of space." We would be exhilarated and excited. We would gasp at the wideness of the horizons, at the limitlessness of places to explore.

Religion, I have been trying to say, was not meant to build prisons but to set us free. It was not meant to inhibit our response to the world, but to facilitate it, to evoke it, to give it a means of expression. That man has misunderstood the gospel who has read it as a summons to a tight and narrow existence, excluding the mystery and marvel of creation. It is, on the contrary, an invitation to see the creation anew, to feel it in all one's bones and organs, to react to it and interact with it, and, most exciting of all, to participate in its *re*creation, which act takes place all the time. It is a great pity that many of the most religious persons one knows are also the stuffiest and unhappiest; this is so likely to dissuade the casual viewer from any real interest in religion.

The truth is that religion, when it is real and vital, is in the nature of a great adventure. It organizes occasional excursions for us into the mostly uncharted realms of spirit and meaning. But it does not confine us to those organized excursions. We are free to wander about on our own and turn up interesting things for ourselves. In this sense, religion—true religion, not that spurious, prepackaged kind—acts to increase one's joy, because it confronts him with the immensity of the universe. It stands him once more before the heterogeneity of creation and bids him marvel at it. It reminds him of the finitude of his own life—of his limitations in time and space and impression—and opens all his vistas again.

This is what religion is really about. It is not interested in peanuts; it is interested in grandeur. And therefore it is able to increase our joy almost unbearably.

As Nels Ferré wrote in *Making Religion Real*, "Religion is real in proportion to its being a living religion. It is right insofar as it helps life and wrong insofar as it hurts it. The final test for making religion real is therefore life itself. If religion is relation to reality and if right religion makes us real, religion and life are at bottom the same."[4]

This is the premise we have been proceeding on—that "religion and life are at bottom the same." And it is the reason the gospel of Jesus Christ is so important, because it is essentially a gospel of freedom, a gospel that frees man from religion in order to live, to discover himself and his universe. It is in these discoveries that he unwittingly discovers God too, for God is always found out of the corner of the eye, never by a direct approach. There is something about God that resists a frontal assault. *He* discovers us. At the moment when we forget him, when we concentrate on the wonders of the earth, on the glories of the creation, he surprises us by being there.

This is why I have emphasized the importance of being human. Because we perceive God in terms of our own perceptual and organizing apparatus, and not merely in terms of who he is in himself, we enhance our ability to see him, to feel him, to celebrate his presence, as we deepen and enrich our own capacities for being who we are. Whatever makes us more human makes God more accessible to us. It is an indirect route, to be sure; but in the final analysis it is the only way. Nothing else so prepares us for recognizing what is holy and eternal in our midst. One might almost exhort his fellowmen, "For *God's* sake, be human."

---

[4] Nels F. S. Ferré *Making Religion Real* (New York: Harper and Row, Publishers, Inc., 1955), p. 138.